JEFFREY A. HARRISON

The Full-Cycle Minute

A Construct in Peak Sales Performance

Systematically evaluate your beliefs and behaviors to help you evolve into the individual and salesperson you desire to be!

Jeffrey A. Harrison
San Diego, California
USA

+1 (858) 736-9997
harjeffrey@gmail.com
www.jeffreyaharrison.com

The author of this book, Jeffrey A. Harrison, has provided information and techniques to help you achieve a better understanding of sales and the selling process. He is dispensing neither business nor psychological advice. The author and publisher take no responsibility for the manner in which this information is utilized, nor do they assume liability for any actions or for the results of those actions, which you may take as a result of the information herein contained.

Cover Design by Kitty McGee

To my beautiful Katelyn Marie
The most wonderfully caring and encouraging daughter
An exceptional student of life and humanity
A patient and thoughtful teacher for her students and me

You have graced my life
You have added purpose and meaning
You have given me great delight

I love you with more energy than the Sun
With more luminance than a Full Moon
And with more abundance than the Earth

Always

Introduction

The Full-Cycle Minute - A Construct in Peak Sales Performance
delivers and examines two personal development models, The Full-Cycle Minute Model and the Personal Foundation Model. These
models deliver a practiced processes that will enrich your life,
strengthen your inner self, redefine personal relationships, and
increase your selling and sales performance and success while giving
you a confidence and peace of mind.

Does your profession performance, relationships and sales goals
suffer because your reaction or response depends on the situation?
Are you tired of trying to fit in by compromising? Have you ever
wondered how your character, integrity, ethics, attitude, behavior
and personal belief system impacts your life and your selling efforts
on a daily basis?

Perhaps you have suffered from personal compromise, self-deception, bad habits, bad decisions and poor choices that may have
buried your authentic self so deep you may not recognize yourself.
Now you're asking; "Where did "I" go?" or "How did I get here?"
How can I get back to the person I was once, my authentic self?

In any of these cases a helpful, sometimes painful, yet very powerful
self-evaluation is in order to reconnect to your authentic self. To do
that you need to take the first step with complete honesty and
honestly look at your character as reflected by your behavior.

This honesty can open your mind to endless possibilities, open your
heart to compassion and open your emotions to joy and happiness.
Your honesty allows you to move forward toward your authentic
self.

An honorable character is the backbone of your true nature, thinking
and emotions that directly affects your behavior, attitude and
performance.

Until now there has been no demonstrated, repeatable process to help develop your character, re-visit your belief system or calibrated new information to help develop your true nature.

Today there is… *The Full-Cycle Minute - A Construct in Peak Sales Performance.*

Peak sales performance requires accomplished disciplines across many diverse professional practices and personal beliefs based in character as well as a knowledge base. The combination and melding of these disciplines are challenged daily and in many cases nothing is more challenging than the development of character which guides all of our spiritual and human encounters.

A healthy character is the underlying foundation effecting a successful selling environment. This sales environment is competitive, aggressive and even cutthroat; presenting you a situational challenge that may bring into contention your current character beliefs that may not serve your authentic self.

Coach John Wooden said *"Be more concerned with your character than your reputation, because your character is what you really are, while your reputation is merely what others think you are."*

Coach Wooden also said *"Success is peace of mind which is a direct result of self-satisfaction in knowing you did your best to become the best you are capable of becoming."*

The Full-Cycle Minute - A Construct in Peak Sales Performance will guide you through two uniquely successful models and processes necessary to become your "best" by understanding you have choices.

Applying those choices require doing the work that directs you towards your peak sales performance. In order to change we need to leave behind some of our past thinking and old ways of thinking to gain new, effective tools geared towards an evolved journey.

Joel Osteen said *"There is a great future in front of you; you can leave your past behind."*

The Full-Cycle Minute - A Construct in Peak Sales Performance provides a unique detailed process to help you evolve into the person you're meant to be while accomplishing the peak sales performance you've always desired.

The book has taken form from my many years of experiences, failures and successes to help you gain an insight to a deliberate process, by taking personal responsibility of conscious choices to evolve. Using the defined modeled process will enhance and effectively engage the sales environment and your world.

You now have the modeled processes in this book that will set the direction to becoming a powerfully motivated participant while evolving into your personal best. You can affect your life and the selling outcome by doing your best, every time.

When you use these performance models you will become focused on the driver for success… You.

There is no shortcut to success yet there are tidbits of wisdom, shared experience and now a modeled platform to establish a means to calibrate today and tomorrow. Practice these models and you will be astonished at your results.

Thank You…

I'd like to thank Katelyn Meier, Jim Cronin, James Kahn and Paul Joyce for your unending support and encouragement.

A special thank you to Cal Prather for without your professional resolve and kind guidance I might never have gotten to this point in life.

The Full-Cycle Minute
A Construct for Peak Sales Performance

TABLE OF CONTENTS

Preface

This book contains my opinions and career experience regarding marketing, sales and selling activities that effect peak sales performance.

The experiences and the processes referenced in this book are all transferable sales skills that can be applied to any or all sales positions from Real Estate, Software and Services Industry, Hard Goods and Retail sales positions.

Selling skills and sales processes as well as best practices are all transferable between sales jobs, industries and professional stations.

I was introduced to the marketing and sales processes 35 years ago while working for various high-tech electronics manufacturers and the services industries.

After my college graduation I began my sales career as an inside sales engineer and rapidly moved into various management positions, including Regional Sales Manager, National Sales Manager, Advertising Manager and Marketing Manager.

Later in my career, I was selected for various senior-level management positions, including General Manager and Vice President of Sales and Marketing. These positions required division responsibility, strategic planning and preparation and close interface with the board of directors. This charge gave me a completely different perspective from which to observe and evaluate corporate operational excellence, sales and marketing strategies and tactics, product development and distribution.

During those years, I was exposed to the hands-on of true strategic marketing process, sales and distribution challenges, and the product development disciplines, including managing product life-cycles.

The biggest challenge by far is the selling aspect of product delivery and revenue generation. There is an old saying, "Anyone can make a product but not anyone can sell it," it held true then as it does today.

I have also spent periods of time as an entrepreneur, pursuing the dream of running a small high-tech advertising agency as well as being a product designer and a book publisher, yet I found myself back in corporate America within several years.

Once I returned I held several outside local sales positions for national companies in various industries; telecommunications, software, hard goods, services, newspaper advertising and technical sales. Most positions were business-to-business yet some were associated with retailers wanting a business revenue stream.

Immersing myself in the sales and selling environment has provided a broader understanding of industry-specific selling processes and procedures yet the basic selling processes are transferable across multiple industries. I spent several years with AT&T, MCI, and other telecommunications companies as an Account Executive and Major Account Manager.

My exposure within established sales departments as a participant and manager has revealed insight to sales procedures, best practices, effective sales management as well as inefficiencies, ineffectiveness, and lack of focus to accomplish successful sustainable performance.

My time in the sales discipline and through my experiences in the product development and marketing process, I've been exposed to many different sales philosophies, concepts, processes, and expectations surrounding the selling event and have come to understand the dynamics of successful selling criteria. It's through my history of managing the selling function that I came up with the concept of *The Full-Cycle Minute – A Construct of Peak Sales Performance.*

At the core of any selling opportunity is the salesperson. I find it odd that no one really looked at or designed a coaching process for salespersons' internal processes, personal belief system, interpersonal communication skills, or general attitude toward working and success in the selling environment. Every selling event begins and ends with the salesperson, period.

The development of The Full-Cycle Minute model becomes a useful tool for your Personal Foundation as a continuous self-adjusting rhythm to help facilitate the desired changes.

It's important to process your experiences in life and in the selling situation to continuously evaluate your personal beliefs against your performance. Understanding how your beliefs, strengths and weaknesses associated with an event affect the outcome and is a key to success.

Once you are aware, you can affect your evolution and your personal mindset—and you are on the road to peak sales performance. Using The Full-Cycle Minute model will deliver a process of empowering meaningful growth.

You are really the only constant in your selling process, so it's important to ground yourself in your own excellence. Yes, the company and its products or services give consistency in the deliverables provided, but you, and only you, are responsible for obtaining an evolved, successful sale completion.

You are the beginning and the end of all that transpires around and within the selling process. Using The Full-Cycle Minute model and believing in yourself generates a creation of empowering cycles that influence the outcome for success.

The Full-Cycle Minute model is a cycle having a beginning and an end, is continuous by nature and re-starting every time you are challenged to think in a different mindset or introduced to new and differing ideas. The process is expanding and evolving constantly.

In these concepts about to be introduce, the only entity I am talking to and about is… You.

The Full-Cycle Minute

A Construct in Peak Sales Performance

To succeed at any venture in life, it is necessary to respect and guide yourself in a manner that evolves and celebrates the uniqueness of your person.

Your family, your immediate friends, your workplace, your education and your outside activities are intricate in the development of your personal best. I believe we all know what in good, we all know what does not serve us and we all know the difference between the two. To develop ourselves on our best efforts will build a solid foundation.

Other key factors in your evolution are influenced by new experiences, new opportunities and new information. Being open to new and potential unknown experiences without predetermined judgments allow the experience to reveal itself without too many filters which broadens your horizons to the newness of each moment.

No matter how steadfast you are in your knowledge and the commitment of your being, it's imperative to understand that the outside world is constantly challenging you to release yourself to societal norms and pressures.

The world challenges you to stretch and explore new thinking through exposure to the many vast personal and social differences life provides. Some take us to an evolved space and some to a diminished places.

These challenges are the catalyst for new re-enforced beliefs or new beginnings, yet as we perceive new worldly encounters, our perception of the world is called to expand, collapse in any event change. If we don't evolve, we are surely stuck.

In most cases, we have a strong will to do what's good with regard to our existing norms and what we have come to know as right or wrong.

Most people are desirous to live life in an evolved space, determined to be the best they can be, every day.

However, when we see others exhibiting less honorable behavior, we may have one of two responses: "I'm glad I don't behave like that" or perhaps, "Well, if they can do it and get away with it, I should be able to as well."

In both instances they agitate our core beliefs and then we are compelled to at least briefly, contemplate, evaluate and judge our own beliefs and behaviors with regard to our observations.

That momentary thinking and resultant decision could change your life forever. It is difficult to be steadfast when others are getting and/or taking what they want by any means possible.

Perhaps in the choice to cheat one does not see the value in their own character or have given up on respect, honor, and integrity within themselves and look to the world for some form of shortcut or an immediate, self-serving success.

If that stream of consciousness occurs by the introduction of worldly activity or the idea of worldly social status quo, it would be helpful to have a process that would help construct, evaluate, and direct your thinking—evolving your best efforts toward your core self and desires.

The Full-Cycle Minute Model

The Full-Cycle Minute is a short five step process which provides guidance for evaluating process leading to informed decision making. By adopting The Full-Cycle Minute model, you can practice a logical process to help evaluate the direction of your thinking and slow down the reaction/response time while evolving subsequent attitudes, ideals and behaviors.

Although the use of the model is a rather quick process, it does require you to assign conscious dedicated time, effort, and energy to fully develop any new or differing process for evolving an informed decision-making process.

The Full-Cycle Minute model is a helpful series of steps to effectively evaluate new ideas, thought-provoking opinions, or even revisit past thinking that perhaps have grown questionable. It's a great impetus to engage your person, world and thinking as a logical pretense to decision making and to personally evolve.

The Full-Cycle Minute model is a simple but effective pathway that utilizes your personal attributes to help you implement a highly personalized process. Practicing this model allows you to reach an informed level of understanding, allowing for a fully integrated response to events, ideas or words that stir either emotional feelings or intellectual activity.

The Full-Cycle Minute model uses your character, ethics, morals, honesty, spirituality, humanity, experiences, and education as baseline criteria helping filter the events that flow through your life. Knowing who you are in relationship to the aforementioned qualities is essential for growth and evolution.

We will discuss later how this model integrates on an ongoing basis within the selling and sales process while strengthening your sales integrity helping attaining peak sales performance.

Moving forward, the reference to character, integrity, ethics, morals, decency, honesty, spirituality and humanity will be reflected by a definitive phrase, Personal Foundation. More detail regarding the Personal Foundation will be discussed in the following sections.

Let's take a look at the specific dynamics of The Full-Cycle Minute model, which has five separate phases that make up the process effecting your evolution.

The Full-Cycle Minute Model

1 - Event (stimulus) - An event occurs, an internal dialogue develops or you hear an idea that triggers your attention because it touches a feeling or an interest you would like to pursue. Your response may be, "Wow, that's interesting," "Oh, that's something I haven't heard or thought of" or "Ouch that hit a nerve." This stirring helps you become aware that there may be foreign ideas, buried feelings or an awakening that makes you aware of a new idea, a different way of thinking or perhaps a new direction to be discovered. An awareness now touches you intuition to investigate.

2 - Awareness (mindfulness) - After the event, an "Ah Ha" moment may occur in your thinking, your intuitive self or feelings, and you may become aware of other options, beliefs, facts, information or others' facets to your current thinking. And through your intuitive nature you may experience a desire to look further into the newness of your thoughts.

Additionally, by looking at these differences, it may affect you and your worldly view as well as views of others. Being aware is being alive. Start to investigate and be open to the journey.

3 - Investigate (clarification) - Your awareness has peaked your interest, starting the evaluation process. Take the time and effort to assimilate your thoughts and explore as needed a more focused exploration of this new information by using other resources for validation.

It's also beneficial to seek counsel from those you respect and honor to help clarify any number of questions. Through your investigation and inquiries, you may find the idea you are uncovering may make perfect sense or no sense at all. You may either adopt your findings as something new and useful or dismiss them altogether. With either choice, a form of acceptance will occur.

4 - Acceptance (acknowledgment) - Now that your investigation has delivered a result and you are satisfied that you have enough information to make an informed decision, you are now able to make a choice. You may either own it as a new belief, thus moving forward and applying it to your Personal Foundation and principles, or you may reject it; file it away as a non-useful event that will not be part of your experiences, but exists as an experience only. Both ownership and rejection are forms of acceptance.

5 - Integration (assimilation) - Incorporate the results into your thinking and your life, both personal and professional. This may be more difficult than expected because we are creatures of habit. You change a habit over a period of time so if you slip, acknowledge it, stand up and start once again.

Evolving

Evolving to provide a broader version and vision of your personal development, spiritual awareness and continuous adjustments of instituting change is the core function of The Full-Cycle Minute model. I believe the human being and spirit have a choice to make, whether to continually evolve or mature.

Maturing has a life expectancy or perhaps a planned obsolescence of reaching a specific destiny, which at that point has an ending. Additionally, maturity is something that is fully developed by definition. If this definition is accurate, I refuse to mature.

I would rather choose to evolve in a continuum of ongoing consciousness to enhance my stay on the planet, rather than believe I will become fully developed at a preconceived time, should be developed by an arbitrary point, or have an expiration date other than my departure.

Evolving is perhaps a foreign way of choosing to look at your life without a destination, unlike the maturing concept which has a destination. This choice and through all other choices we are in charge of only the direction of the outcome; not the outcome itself or any other outcome.

That is why it's so important to understand what you are in charge of and not in control of. It's the moment and the choice that we are in charge of, we are not in control of anything. We simple are not that powerful to control any outcome.

Every moment is filled with choices. You desire certain outcomes so make the choices that will move you closer to those desires.

I also believe that with an evolving mentality, your professional life, your personal life, your relationships, and your destiny will be better served by this open mentality. Choose to evolve and refuse to mature. Make good choices.

Using the Model

The choice concept is exactly the type of process and forward thinking that are characteristic of The Full-Cycle Minute model.

Although this model is simplistic in nature, if given serious attention and consideration, its steps could be the backbone to your new evolved personal and professional life.

Most thinking starts from an external experience, a stimuli, a feeling or an internal dialogue. It's from this event point that we start.

Forward Thinking

Forward thinking is the idea of taking the time to review your current solution set or thinking, before you choose, to a forward looking moment and envision an outcome over each choice. This allows the moment a momentary "freeze frame" for you to project your choices and then take action on that choice. It can happen in nanoseconds once you develop the technique.

Forward thinking, once synthesized through this model, will begin to affect other beliefs, thoughts, ideas, and behavior as well and have an effect on similar or other opposing ideas because you now believe in your choice and now choose what you allow in or keep out.

One change in thinking may disturb other beliefs and opinions, causing a personal course change during which you feel the effects of evolving. When future events occur, The Full-Cycle Minute model is ready to be used as a quick definitive tool, providing a process for an evolved outcome by taking action to engage your choices.

Reality vs. Clarity

You would be surprised at the number of people who take in a proven fact and dismiss it because it isn't part of their immediate core thinking, belief system, knowledge base or their value system. Are they just stubborn or are they protecting themselves and fearful of being found out that perhaps they don't know everything?

Yet others take in deceptive and fraudulent information and will hold it as the fact because they heard it on TV, received a friend's opinion or because a pseudo authority figure deems it so. Are they fearful of looking misinformed, out of touch or just stupid - adhering their thinking to any passing thought?

In either case, there is no desire to validate any of these scenarios through investigation. It's a true disaster awaiting to happen. To be lead sheepishly through life without validating what is presented to you or what you come to believe is extremely dangerous.

Slowing Down

Perhaps the single biggest takeaway is to slow down our fast-paced days and be present in every moment and encounter. Pay attention to your massagers, sources, events your intuition not outside minutia. Slow down enough to allow this process to reveal your authentic self within the moment. Trust yourself and be heard.

Supporting your decision to further evolve by always using your intuition to clarify your minds direction and engage your spiritual self will serve as a healthy compass.

The path to evolving is slowing down enough to engage, drink in, taste, smell, hear and imagine your life as it delivers you opportunities and challenges to become the best person you can be and to obtain and sustain your peak performance.

This model incorporates a process to help you continually evaluate your beliefs, your feelings, your knowledge base, your opinions and your resulting behaviors. The Full-Cycle Minute model also helps you systematically evaluate your beliefs and behaviors to help you evolve into the individual and salesperson you desire to be.

Applying the Model to Selling and Sales

This concept can apply to all situations you encounter within your personal life and your professional sales life.

The model will further help you gain new momentum when applying it to your sales disciplines. In every selling encounter, there is an opportunity to hear a new idea and listen to new information, and by practicing this model you will bring discipline to your evaluation and learning process.

In every business or company environment, there are numerous exchanges of information that require understanding and clarity with an openness to realize the diversity of thinking and ideas.

If new or foreign ideas reveal themselves, use The Full-Cycle Minute model to quickly evaluate and extrapolate fact from fiction. If the fact can't be verified on the spot, take it up later when you're able to complete the cycle. You are not compelled to take a position or stand until you are ready.

In every selling situation, where gaining a competitive advantage requires communication, exchange of needs and wants, or a results-based performance, there is a place for The Full-Cycle Minute model.

With the ability to effectively practice this concept and enhance or evolve your thinking, this internal processing of The Full-Cycle Minute model will result in positive effects on your personal life and behavior. By adopting these processes, you will find a resurgence of evolving your choices and in turn providing a pathway to success by being present.

When you are present you are aware, awareness engages evaluation, and when you evaluate, you will acquire a result that either enhances your life or is put away as not being relevant to your Personal Foundation.

Although the world is spinning around you chaotically and it would like to define you in its own terms by worldly and societal norms, it's your responsibility to stand fast in your Personal Foundation and use your choices to move either in concordance or opposition.

The Full-Cycle Minute model will help you renew and evolve your Personal Foundation to not only meet your personal evolving desires, but also send a worldly statement giving a clear rendition of who you are.

It may take a little time over several instances, some repetition, and much practice to incorporate this new awareness and actionable change into your Personal Foundation. Your dedication to this process will result in a solid foundation, based in an actionable process, and will deliver consistent behavior and outcome in accordance with your authentic self. Be patient.

Your Personal Foundation

Before we get started on the Personal Foundation model, it's imperative to understand that moving forward there is a basic premise that this concept is built upon. It is my belief that we are spirits having a human experience and not humans having a spiritual experience. Without any sense of spirituality, the world can run us over, leaving us listless, unengaged and untethered.

Personal Foundation Model

Character-Spirituality

The primary footing of the Personal Foundation model is your character which is closely tied if not oriented toward and anchored in your spirituality. The spirit is a conscious, incorporeal being as opposed to matter and is a vital principle in human beings.

In my definition spirituality is not based in any organized religion, cult or following yet is a personal connection between you and your belief in a creator, a higher power or the energy of the universe.

An engaged spirit is essential for a healthy and balanced life. In our Personal Foundation of core beliefs and of self, the spirit is the ultimate purveyor of the necessary positive energy and influencers running through those beliefs and thoughts. In many cases, it appears within us as an intuitive moment, a knowing without a worldly frame or through an unbound internal idea.

The content of the elements of our Personal Foundation are continually being synthesized by and through the spirit, which enables us to revisit personal and worldly issues with a divine consciousness.

Our spiritual connection is without worldly physicality, yet it provides us with a divine compass—always guiding, always aware, always available and always reliable. We just need to slow down to engage it. This consciousness sometimes goes unheard because of too much activity, too much noise or it's heard and not abided by, which plays out in all case, a choice.

When this consciousness or intuition goes unattended, it could very well be there is too much noise, chaos, confusion, or minutia around us and we just need to slow down. The need for calm and quiet moments throughout the day is essential to maintain connectivity to our divine consciousness, ultimately providing the needed balance for our humanity.

The knowing and intuition of the spirit is grounded in the premise of an external higher power or purveyor of our internal spiritual compass. We either choose to accept this notion and honor it with synergy or we choose to move through life ignoring it, sometimes untethered, aimless, unfulfilled and perhaps directionless.

Your spirituality aspect is essential for sales integrity and can enable you to achieve a high level of peak sales performance by displaying your character in personal interaction with your prospects.

As a sales professional, when you're in highly competitive surroundings, having a healthy spiritual footing, sound character and a developed ethical compass facilitates an honest and humane relationship with your prospects, yourself, and your work environment. This creates a safe environment enabling a free-flowing exchange of information, ideas and creates a win-win atmosphere.

Additionally, the spirit serves as a resource for energy and renewal that's necessary for the high-energy consuming sales professional. This connection provides a sense that you're not alone; you have a confidant who believes in you and your abilities. When your character and spirit are balanced with your intellect and personality, the outward demeanor of your person reveals a peacefulness that's noticed by others.

Prospects are attracted to these characteristics and desire to conduct business with salespeople of character who have knowledge and tranquility that transcends the event.

The lifeblood of the positive energy that you feel flowing through your body is the awareness of spirit. Again, the spirit is not tied to any religion; it's present in everyone and is connected to a higher power, known to many as the creator, God. This connection provides us a sense of belonging and a sense of community, and it's satisfied through intuition, self-awareness, love, compassion, grace, and humility.

The next set of building blocks in the Personal Foundation model is comprised of integrity, ethics, morals, and education taking form as character.

Characters' Building Blocks

As you know, character is generally defined by integrity, ethics, and morals, and I have added evolved and enhanced continuous knowledge and education.

As a person whose livelihood is one of the oldest professions on the planet, you know that one of the most important sales tool in the selling dynamics includes the assessment of personal character when dealing with prospects. It is not only you assessing them; they are assessing you as well.

Whether that assessment is determined by a short or brief interaction with the potential prospect or a complete selling process, you can be assured a character evaluation is underway, on both sides.

Let's take a look at a couple of the elements within the character profile that play a large role in the selling environment and are evaluated at moment one.

Integrity

The adherence to moral and ethical principles such as honesty, fact and trust are the cornerstones to integrity. Unlike your eyes or the nose on your face, integrity bears no physicality other than action.

The outward manifestation of integrity shows up in your behavior, your personality, your words and your attitudes. Most people have sensitivity when it comes to perceiving another's integrity and it typically reveals itself as perceived inconsistency. That is, saying one thing and behaving another, lying and getting caught or a series of misstatements, fabrications or exaggerations.

Without integrity, there is no real connection to your humanity or to your authentic self. Within the sales discipline and the selling environment and process, it is imperative to lead with integrity to affect a just result.

Ethics

Personal and professional ethics are an important ingredient in the successful selling process. They are reflected as a rule of conduct recognized with respect to a particular class of human interactions and or particular groups or cultures (business ethics, medical ethics or religious ethics), including moral principles. Personal and professional ethics are important ingredients in a successful selling process.

This code of conduct is standardized on basic human desires; a platform of fairness, decency, respect and equality. Application of ethics at every level of human interaction, both personal and professional, helps maintain equilibrium in self and society. Honoring and practicing these principles is essential to achieve your humanity and it enhances peak sales performance.

A high ethical benchmark guarantees integrity in any transaction and eliminates any potential sense of wrongdoing while building trust and mutual respect.

Without a high ethical standard, it may become attractive to interact with others using compromised or situational ethics. The result of unethical behavior results in a sense of fear of being discovered, compromised authenticity, and distrust which continually plagues the thinking.

These characteristics are emitted by your person as energy and can be sensed by others through awkward behavior, body language and inconsistent speech patterns or just general nervousness.

Ethical consistency is important for you and your prospect; if you don't have it, the result will be an internal struggle with your Personal Foundation and your interaction with prospects.
This struggle may reveal itself to others by their perception of your inconsistencies through your behavior.

People who pay attention are perceptive of any inconsistencies and upon noticing them, will discount much if not all of your actions or words and may choose to disassociate themselves entirely. They will shy away from conducting business with you and give various reasons and excuses for their decision.

Morals

Morals pertain to or are concerned with the principles or rules of right conduct or the distinction between right and wrong. They convey fact or counsel as to right conduct rather than on legalities, enactment, or custom as a moral obligation.

By conducting yourself morally and subscribing to and practicing under these fundamental characteristics, the interactions and exchange of information, ideas or solutions in any interaction will help facilitate honest and factual exchanges and communication.

It is imperative that sales professionals take the highest ground when it comes to conducting business transactions with character. Your conduct is under the highest scrutiny and an essential element when prospects make decisions to conduct business with you.

Your behavior of evolved character will resonate throughout your interactions and serve as a beacon to the people with whom you conduct business—and it will result in you receiving positive accolades as a person of character and integrity.

In cases when it's difficult to sustain your moral practice and standards because a person or prospect requests or suggests a compromise during a business transaction, it may be just as well to walk away from that type of business rather than compromise your character.

Education

Your formal and informal education, life's education and collective experience is an important element and a fundamental ingredient to your Personal Foundation. It is very important to continuously educate yourself on all matters that interest and effect you as well as the getting the education required for developing your skills. Education helps to broaden your horizons, evolve your perspective and deepen your understanding of life; personally, socially, and professionally.

Most people have successfully achieved a base education through the 12th grade and have graduated. Typically, this is just the beginning of a long interesting journey of education, knowledge and excellence. That journey will take many different forms and pathways and is never the same for any two people.

Recognizing that people learn in many different ways and differing venues allows for educational growth through many varied curriculums. That being said, it is essential to evaluate how you learn and which venue serves you best. Is it by reading information, attending a lecture, listening, hands-on or actually participating in an event under instruction?

There is a misnomer running amok that a higher education is essential for successful in the professional business environment.

In many cases it is helpful but usually not essential to have a professional business career. If you plan to reach mid-management positions and higher, it will be very helpful to understand that this career path usually requires a higher education.

A key component in educating yourself is the desire to learn and develop your education fortress and grow your expertise on any topics or subjects you desire. A desire to deliver peak sales performance and professional excellence requires continuous education and a quest for knowledge.

Knowledge Base

Essential to growing this portion of your Personal Foundation is also a healthy desire to continually grow your knowledge base and develop and learn sophisticated business concepts and solution processes. Whether it's specific to your career, related to business interests or just to satisfy your inquisitive nature, follow your desires. Any continued education will benefit you, your prospects and the planet.

You cannot have enough education to compete in the highly competitive business environment and specifically the professional sales arena. The unique thing about sales is that it is a highly competitive field and you are continually on display, so staying abreast of trending information and relevant processes are essential.

Your visibility within your company and the outside competitive business world creates an enormous amount of stress to keep your edge by learning and applying current knowledge to your everyday activities.

Your peers will push you by their knowledge growth and continual education efforts to gain a competitive advantage. This should stimulate you to push yourself to maintain an educational advantage that challenges your professional desires and your competition. Your education is one of the tools that needs sharpening on a continuous basis.

Education can take the form of a college degree as well as outside continuing education. Other avenues include extension or evening classes, professional seminars and attending informative lectures.

Extra Curriculum

Lectures given at local universities and colleges as well as sponsored professional gatherings and trade shows of various vertical industry leaders are great resource.

These types of events are also good for your profession by helping you make new networking contacts outside your normal sales practice. Events of this nature tend to re-energize your enthusiasm by meeting new people under new conditions and providing a different orientation for your networking and selling efforts.

By stepping out to these events and perhaps outside of your comfort zone, a whole new energy of people wanting to extend their personal experiences and their knowledge to further heighten their professionalism awaits. It's all part of your learning process and education.

Additionally, online courses are another excellent way to broaden your educational base. An occasional visit to the World Wide Web or YouTube with a search by a specific topic will yield a plethora of interesting and perhaps informative information via written articles, audio and videos. Take advantage of this free opportunity and varied media to continuously build your knowledge base. Don't forget to calibrate and verify information for facts, not opinion or unfound truths.

Remembering that anything worthwhile requires the investment of time, invest your time wisely by fulfilling your desire and embracing your interests; don't ignore them.

Self-development takes many shapes and forms and should not be fashioned by limiting your available time. Set aside time to engage weekly in your desires to achieve your educational goals and learning the necessary information to become an authority within your selling scenarios.

Take the time to seize potential opportunities that are presented to you to build a broader educational foundation.

Exploration by searching is a wonderful adventure that can provide extremely high-yield results and enjoyment. The biggest thing you can do for yourself is to take action once you're stirred or directed by your interests; that is a necessary ingredient to build a sustainable knowledge base.

Core Beliefs

Over the course of your life's development, your personal belief system has been constantly evolving. You have spent a lifetime gathering experiences, information and knowledge through a myriad of ways.

Your core belief system resides deep within you at both the spiritual and human being level and is imprinted on you at a very early age.

Influence on your core beliefs is continually being exerted, challenged or reinforced by general conversations, receiving opinions of others, personal experiences, stories as well as education.

You have learned a process to help you evaluate incoming information to either dismiss it or accept it with your own process.

One of the intentions of The Full-Cycle Minute and Personal Foundation model is to deliver a broader perhaps more detailed process that you may relate to and desire to incorporate. However, like most new ideas, you may choose to modify or change this model to either intensify the process or scale it to fit your current system of processing. Try to keep the underlying concept intact.

Your personal and professional belief systems work in conjunction with your intuitive self, so make sure you listen to your intuition when you are conducting interactions with people, prospects and business opportunities. As I mentioned before, that little voice needs your attention.

A strong core belief system will serve you as a professional salesperson who uses honest and true information, facts, knowledge, understanding and trust to gain credibility in the selling environment. Your core beliefs are rooted deeply in your history and have depth that offers a perspective into your personal identity that nothing else can provide. Honor that as you evolve.

Influences on Your Foundation

There are four additional important impactful influences within your life that have a profound importance and effect on your evolution and growth. Your family, your friends, your colleagues and most importantly your expectations. The aforementioned people are your special confidants and typically represent safe, long-term relationships that have perhaps provided counsel in the past.

These groups have an understanding of the majority of your authentic self. Additionally, they are probably the most safe and free to speak with you delivering candor and openness. These are great assets to continue to cultivate and nurture during your days on the planet.

The most significant influence, one that can be extremely harsh on us, is our own expectations. Expectations are a completely different animal. They can be the curse that delivers us into disappointment or they can drive us to think we have an unsubstantiated predetermined outcome that is completely ungovernable and most likely false.

To reveal an event's outcome, some form of action needs to occur not just wishing or dreaming it so.

Thus, don't fantasize an unsubstantiated and perceived outcome until you have taken action in the direction of success. If you don't take action, how can your expectations or anything for that matter become an outcome?

Take the actions necessary, let life reveal itself by doing, and don't ruin the outcome due to misdirected expectations and the anticipation of things not yet materialized. If you expect a certain outcome without action, there is a high likelihood you will be unfulfilled and disappointed.

It's essential to remove from your expectations the idea of "I want from" and replace it with "I'm willing to give."

In the selling environment, when you give maximum effort to your preparation and deliver your best, your actions will reveal the prospect's response (outcome), not necessarily your expectation.

Trust

Trust is an important ingredient in building your personal foundation. Trusting in yourself to do your best possible work is critical to achieving evolved peak sales performance. Trust in yourself, your judgment and your intuition to guide you through the selling process and any difficult circumstances. And trust your team.

It's also important to gain trust with the prospect so the selling process has every opportunity to be successful. This begins by listening wisely to what is being spoken while evaluating it against your beliefs and knowledge. As the relationship moves forward and mutual respect develops, meaningful exchanges of information and ideas begin to occur and a health relationship is now started.

When prospects trust you, as well as your products, services and company, you're much better positioned to satisfy their requirements.

In the event that a situation arises that needs resolution, be forthright and honest. Once your integrity standard is set by your actions, prospects can trust you to deliver what you say you can deliver, the best possible solution.

It goes without saying to never betray a prospect's trust and always error on the side of under-committing and over-delivering.

Humanity

Humanity consists of human constructs and concerns as opposed to natural processes. Inclusive is the entirety of our social relations, both personal and professional. In short, humanity is how we treat one another, and all living things.

To treat others with decency and respect, it is imperative that we treat ourselves in the same manner.

We learn our humanity by the very nature of our spirit and our being from birth and by observing it in others. These observed experiences can be integrated into your Personal Foundation.

The old saying, "to love someone else you need to be able to love yourself" is very true. It is from that point of departure that internal emotional change is necessary to effect any behavioral and outward change.

Be aware that your thinking may trick you into believing the problem is always out there, not within. When you believe the world is the problem, you are essentially removing yourself from the world, when in actuality you are part of that world, therefore part of the problem. Believing it's the world, you may begin to follow the crowd and take no personal responsibility for your own actions, direction and results, always assigning blame elsewhere.

Take personal responsibility and engage your humanity.

When you're sitting across from a personal friend or prospect, your compassion and humanity may help you better understand their behavior. Be observant, be diligent and be compassionate.

Have the grace to give the benefit of the doubt and clarify to fully understand any given situation.

Intuition

The intuition that speaks to you by way of an internal dialogue, or a stirring of feelings is an indicator that some form of attention is needed and it should not be ignored.

These stirrings, although not immediately evident, for whatever reason, require your attention, so pay attention to them.

To fully understand an event that has moved you, take the time to understand what may have just occurred prior to these feelings or stirrings and address it immediately if possible.

If that's not immediately undertaken, make a mental note to revisit it later. Just the fact that you are aware of an event that has moved you indicates you are in the moment, and available, so don't lose the opportunity to capture the moment.

Intuitive Events

If you are an emotional or a reactionary-type person, I would highly suggest you error on the side of becoming less reactionary.
You can do this by making mental or even written notes and allowing yourself time to process what actually occurred, removing the emotion and not overreacting.

In such cases, there's a need to evaluate what was actually said or what actually happened, and how it stirred you internally. It may have triggered some unresolved issues that may have nothing to do with the event or it may stem from the immediate actual interaction. Rest assured that whatever it is, it is unresolved.

Take the time to fully understand what triggered your intuition before you take action to resolve it.

In your personal or business life, when it comes to interpersonal relationships, it may become difficult to deal with these intuitions, for they may cause unwanted or unneeded tension between you and the other person.

Sometimes we won't challenge what stirs our intuition or feelings because if that irritates the situation, a conflict could be created. And, most people typically like to avoid conflict at all costs.

Honesty in relationships is extremely important, so to engage a person-to-person interaction or response to your intuitiveness, make sure you go at it with kindness and love. The last thing you need to do is appear hostile or even critical.

Remember that great communication starts with listening. It is also imperative not to take things personally, although they may be; look at it from a higher ground to gain perspective.

If it is personal and you own it, it's healthy to acknowledge that. It not only helps you grow as a person, but also increases your confidence by demonstrating your awareness of self-development. Any and all exchanges are opportunities to evolve and sometimes evolution is painful.

When you're dealing with prospects you will, from time to time, have your intuition stirred. At that point, the best thing you can do is understand what's moving around within you as well as how much of it is your own issue and what is actually coming from and owned by your prospect.

Make sure what is being agitated is pertinent to the selling process and the current situation, and if so, work on clarifying to help remove the discomfort by an open and honest communication. Ask those clarifying questions.

Honesty

The preliminary element that is most important in honesty is with yourself. It is imperative, throughout your many personal and business interactions, to recognize the underlying need to be brutally honesty with yourself.

If you're unable to be truthful with yourself than honesty with others will be difficult as well.

With regard to your personal honesty and your personal and professional performance it's your ability to honestly fulfill the needs of your prospect that take priority. Honesty, especially in communication is extremely important.

Sometimes it is painful to face your personal "less-than-honest" demons head-on, yet to evolve your Personal Foundation it is extremely necessary: to thy own self be true. Once you're able to practice that, honesty becomes easier to practice with others.

Helpfulness

As a salesperson, one of the necessary attributes for your success is your ability to help prospects realize their needs. The spirit of helpfulness nourishes and ties you not only to your desired outcome and humanity, but more importantly, your spirituality. Being helpful in any manner breeds self-awareness, cultivates love and compassion, develops grace, and displays your humility for prospects and everyone you touch.

When you're helpful to others without designs on an expected outcome, you outwardly engage the very essence of life while creating your own balance. Helping others is critical in your own evolution.

Acknowledging and taking action toward someone else's needs before your own enriches your character and is a continuum to compassion for humanity.

Being mindful of all these characteristics and elements, it's not difficult to fully grasp how dynamic, diverse and volatile your Personal Foundation becomes when you are aware of the complexities of integration.

As you evolve and grow, you will realize that evolving is not only a gift; it becomes an art. And as an artist, you are able to create any scenario you can imagine or dream.

Within the scope of evolution don't forget to dream, and most importantly don't forget to paint that dream—for painting is taking the action of imagining and integrating the lifeblood called spirit.

Know Your Strengths and Weaknesses

It's impossible to know everything. The starting line for any self-improvement is to write down all your strengths and weaknesses before you can begin to understand the complexity of the upcoming work ahead of you. Once that's complete, you can start to address your weaknesses and hone your strengths. A continuous self-assessment of your personal desires and adjustments as well as your business acumen can keep you busy for quite a while. Self-assessment is imperative to be successful at developing your Personal Foundation.

Your ability to be honest with yourself regarding your abilities and desires and to take confident action to strengthen your weaknesses will help you ascend to peak sales performance and the salesperson you choose to be.

Business Acumen

There are many facets to business, including internal company politics and dynamics; the company's financial model, Performa and balance sheets; market trends; misbehaving external financial markets; human resources challenges such as attracting an educated workforce or operating within a restricted pool of talent; and the all-encompassing and unknown positions of our country's and the world's political environment.

Although this seems overwhelming, these elements need to be appreciated and understood to the best of your ability. Ongoing awareness and uninhibited exploration of the aforementioned is part of your ongoing professional growth and education.

This knowledge base demands required and continuous reading to become a consummate professional salesperson.

The more you know and the more you understand, the less likely it is you'll have to try and hit a curveball. I'm not saying that every pitch is a hittable fastball right down the middle of the plate, but when you understand the behavior of what's moving around you or coming at you, you are more likely to be successful.

It's guaranteed that what you learn today will inevitably change, perhaps as soon as tomorrow. You will not wake up one morning and have everything you need with regard to understanding business without a commitment to continue your education. It just doesn't appear; you have to build your knowledge base one day at a time.

Remembering you may not have all the time in the world to dig as deep as you would like, it's critical to have a meaningful understanding in as many areas as possible and be as broad as possible. Having an upfront understanding on as many disciplines as possible supports your ability to engage in your sales opportunity with confidence.

This understanding will help you strategize and develop your sales plan while becoming a successful professional salesperson and preparing for your next step.

The attribute of facing your own issues tenaciously allows you to strengthen your core values, evolve your personal foundation and approach outside honesty issues with the same personal integrity.

Expectations

At best, the expectation you can have is to do your personal best without designs on the outcome.

Expect to do your best, expect to be prepared, and develop the understanding that you have no power over the outcome other than to perform at your highest level. Take control of your best efforts by preparation and understand that's all you have power or control over; empowering yourself to do your personal best. Any untethered expectation of a particular outcome needs to be released and replaced by goal-oriented actions.

One of the bigger caveats to expectations is not having any goals that create healthy expectations.

Set proper and reasonable customer expectations. Set and focus on honest, truthful and reasonable goals, not what you believe will be the expected outcome. Goals with actionable tasks lead to peak performance and most importantly, the actions necessary to successfully complete your desire.

You have no control over the outcome so rid yourself of that unnecessary expectation. Do the work and receive the reward.

Use your Personal Foundation to anchor your goals and not untethered expectations. Be careful to avoid unsolicited expectations of others and develop a realistic understanding of how people, prospects and the world behave when developing goals using their criteria to assign an expectation.

It's important to understand that having an expectation of your abilities doesn't mean the expected result will actually be delivered. It takes hard work, dedication and resolve to deliver your best, so rely on your activity and goal setting to help materialize a committed course of action.

Conversely, we project personal expectations on others that are totally unjust, unwarranted and unrealistic without understanding the others desires. They may have a totally different attitude of your expectation for them that doesn't match their desires. In order to resolve these masques it's incumbent on both parties to have a concise communication and a comprehensive exchange of both sides thoughts, thinking and ideas; not just expectations. By removing expectations an open and concerned dialog results in clear boundaries, respectful concessions and personal space.

It's imperative to have honesty on both all fronts, because to rely on an expectation created in a vacuum without any specific result is unrealistic.

Assumptions

Making assumptions when engaging your prospect is never a good idea. Assumptions should never be engaged, yet alone practiced.

Assumptions are a lazy person's thinking. It's just as easy to get to the answer without assuming, simply asking for more information or input. Get the answer you need by ask the question.

Concluding without any real information and assuming your own beliefs without validation is a recipe for catastrophe. Using your own unfounded pretense of assumption without any useful fact or knowledge your conclusion will inherently be wrong.

Assumptions occur under many conditions:
- being fearful of looking stupid so you quit inquiring
- discounting the person you are talking to as being uniformed or just wrong
- over-talking the sender in a conversation to promote your position while disregarding theirs
- being too lazy to take the time or care about accuracy by not asking questions.

You can dig a deep hole with your prospect when you assume that you have the answer already in your mind without ever asking a single question.

Seek first to understand; then be understood. When you do not seek to understand, you insert your own thinking into prospect or personal interactions without ever checking in with the other side for any accuracy.

You may do this because:
- you either think you know what they're thinking
- you are timid about broaching a possible sensitive subject
- you are fearful of getting an answer you don't want to hear
- you need to maintain control

Any rational for assuming enables a complete misguided event resulting in an unfruitful moments.

To hold the belief that you know what someone else is thinking or you know the answer to that person's thinking reveals a massive ego issue, a problematic trajectory destine for disaster.

Remember, when you engage with another person or prospect you're only half of the conversation, half of the opportunity, half of the problem and half of the solution. Error by checking with the other half.

It's not essential to believe that you have all the answers. Even if you do have answers, it's your responsibility to help lead other people or prospects to their own answers. Through the use of your communication skills and knowledge base use questions that help them see a different perspective or learn a different process and result.

It's better to have them realize where you are coming from rather than have you tell them or dictate their journey to the answer. It's respectful, humble and gracious to lead informative exchanges in this manner.

Master of Your Personal Foundation

As you develop and master these inherent fundamentals in your Personal Foundation, it will be necessary for continued growth to stretch and expand your thinking, process and your evolution.

As you continue to deal with people, add new information and develop your Personal Foundation, it will become noticeable to your relationships who will begin see your evolution and a different experience with your new authentic self.

People enjoy and want to associate and conduct business with integrity and authentic people, especially sales prospects.

Your evolution will also influence and develop your personality as well as your people skills. As you learn to enjoy your personal engagements with others and realize there is learning in all things, building your Personal Foundation becomes a joy not a job.

To conduct successful business and achieve peak sales performance, it is essential to be genuine and sincere. Sincerity requires humility, empathy and sensitivity to the prospects, their business and their personal vulnerabilities. Remember it's not just about you; it's your processes that provide a pleasurable and successful interaction in a powerful and meaningful way.

Satisfying the professional relationship through your personal development is the centerpiece of your success.

Communications

Communicating is a critical part of your job as a salesperson and a human being. There are several aspects to good communication and the most important to peak sales performance is listening, and more importantly, active listening. Yet another revealing type of communiqué during any interaction is body language.

It takes many hours and experiences of interpersonal situations to practice and develop constructive communication skills that yield clear and effective communication. Evolving these skills throughout your life should not be neglected.

Oral Communications

An effective communication tool in your professional salesperson quiver is your ability to listen, listen, and listen. It's not good enough just to hear what someone is saying. You need to be completely engaged and not simultaneously having your own internal dialogue. Sitting there trying to figuring out what you are going to say next, assuming you understand without listening completely and being in a hurry to move on, are telltale signs of ineffective listening. Listening requires your full attention. You will have plenty of time to speak when the situation reveals itself.

By paying strict attention to the speaker, you will receive information, data and insight that you might have otherwise missed. If you are just hearing their words and not present and engaged with what they are telling you, you might as well not be there at all. When you are just hearing and not actively listening to someone, you're probably formulating your response in your head. Active listening will be discussed later in this chapter.

When you really listen, you are able to take away not only the words, meaning of the words, voice inflection, and intention of the speaker, but also that person's understanding, insights and personal position with regard to what is being discussed.

Listening takes:
- your full attention
- undivided attention
- focus
- being present

It is not inhibited by your self-agenda or by wanting to participate by speaking or promoting your ideas. You'll get your chance. It's about you receiving someone else's expression and honoring it by working to clarify and completely understand the person's position or feelings as accurately as possible.

Listening requires removing yourself as an active speaker and engaging the incoming dialogue with all your abilities to actively hear what the sender is saying. When I say actively hear, what I mean is the ability to stay with the current conversation without formulating anything in your mind including opinion, wanting to speak, wanting to share or having a "been there done that" type of knee-jerk internal desire to respond. You as the listener are nonresponsive until speakers have finished their complete thoughts.

The listening portion of a conversation is not about you; it's about the speaker. Your job in the listening mode is to take in what has been said and fully understand what it is you think you heard through the use of clarifying questions. Clarifying what it is you think the person meant by what was said is a key ingredient to understanding.

It seems simple enough, but it takes plenty of practice to quiet the voices in your mind that want to speak out and become part of a conversation.

Conversations are usually two-way, but participating in a conversation with intention requires a certain level of understanding. The intention of the sender is to send accurate thoughts, ideas, knowledge, information and feelings through your communications that can effectively register and/or be understood by the listener.

Again, to do that, you have to be focused on the sender, not yourself.

One of the best ways to display sincerity and develop a mutually beneficial relationship with your prospect or another person is to use your listening skill to gain understanding and mutual respect.

I have heard more people say, "My experience with salespeople is they seem destined to always ... talk." Silence to an excessively talkative salesperson can be problematic; it usually results in nervous chatter or activity that causes a distraction to the process of effective communication.

There is a natural cadence to effective communication. When in conversation, using manageable sentence lengths, concise and focused delivery of singular ideas, along with managed excitement will lead to this natural interaction. Be mindful that there is nothing attractive about a run-on sentence that continues endlessly without any thought, structure or ending.

Typically, strong personalities behave in this manner, perhaps to cover up the fact that quiet and calm do not resonate within them. Remember, it's the silence between the notes that makes the music.

The personalities in a conversation have a lot to do with the type of communication that will transpire. Strong personalities have the need to dominate conversations, perhaps to demonstrate superiority, the need for attention, or they just don't understand how good communication works. The strong personality types with an "I, me, mine" mentality are sometimes guilty of talking excessively, resulting in loss of the listener attention and disengagement of active participation. That usually results in an overwhelming information dump, which is uncomfortable, unnecessary and indecipherable. It's also very uncomfortable and somewhat dismissive when participation in a conversation is difficult.

Basically, the combination of an aggressive personality and an expansive amount of information—relevant or irrelevant—typically results in an overwhelming feeling when combined.

It's much like intimidation or "I have to win" attitude; one-upmanship results in the listener shutting down or concluding any further participation.

If you happen to have this type of personality and need to provide large amounts of information, especially technical data (with unfamiliar terms and clichés), the conversation could be disastrous if your personality overruns the situation. You may make prospects feel uncomfortable or even inadequate because they may not understand what you're saying and what you're saying may be fragmented, or they are unable to engage because of your dominance. As someone with a strong personality, you must be mindful that you could run somebody over if you're not aware of your behavior.

Yet another personality type is the timid, shy type. It's sometimes hard to get anything out of them especially if they have been intimidated or fearful of sounding inept. If this is the case back down your energy and enthusiasm a notch or two and work to make them comfortable. In any case use clarifying questions to open them up the conversation to create an active exchange.

It's important to keep the communication relevant to what the prospect has the capacity to understand. That's why asking open-ended questions is extremely important in the beginning of a conversation to establish some form of baseline knowledge.

To be a good listener, it's necessary to put yourself on the back burner and place the sender front and center while having a somewhat inquisitive and detective-like mentality (either naturally or by design). In some cases, being inquisitive is not a natural condition.

People who are self-centered and narcissistic typically are unconcerned with others' opinions, information, or facts, other than their own. If you run into someone like that, it may be difficult to be heard, but your active listening skills will help you gain headway into a meaningful dialogue. Slowing the interaction down is also effective.

By staying focused and on target with your clarifying questions, a conversational cadence may be established, resulting in a slow and deliberate dialogue.

When you practice this skill set, sometimes a phenomenon occurs when prospects see the effectiveness of your skills and begin to mirror your excellence.

Good questions come from an intrinsic desire, a want and willingness to fully understand another's position or gain further information and insight into the person and the impending relationship.

Identifying prospects' concerns and not assuming anything requires strength and vulnerability of not being a know-it-all showing an evolved openness to listen and learn.

A peak sales performer will explore any and all available communication pathways, knowing that having a robust and meaningful conversation will help develop an effective working relationship as well as mutual respect.

By understanding the complexities of evolved communication you will have a better position for healthy and successful business relationship as well as personal relationships.

Remember, seek first to understand, and then be understood.

Be the salesperson who "listens them into doing business with you." By that, I mean, the more probing and clarifying questions you propose to prospects, a higher yield of agreement and engagement will occur. Being a good listener is important. Being a great active listener is an imperative. This is the greatest characteristic of a professional salesperson. I can't say that too many times: actively listen.

If you're not familiar with active listening, here's a homework assignment: find out more about it.

There are hundreds of books and articles available to help you learn, understand, and develop the strategies and tactics necessary to become a great active listener. I've covered the subject only briefly below.

React or Respond

Sometimes when engaged in conversations, debate or exchange of information and ideas with prospects and even friends we get our emotions ruffled or internally agitated by tone, inference or attitude.

I like to use a technique of responding and not reacting. This allows me to slow down where a charged exchange or a contentious event may be charged with a hidden agenda, pent up emotion or the sender's frustration.

I don't want to react emotionally. In any case I don't want to receive it into myself or take any ownership as my own in any form.

I choose to respond by processing the entirety of the event rather than reacting with untethered emotionally charged feelings. It's important to remember that a reaction is typically connected to an unresolved emotionally charged history, low self-esteem or feelings of less than. A response is a processing technique that acknowledges the emotions that are touched by the words, accepting those feelings in a healthy way while allowing movement towards understanding and hearing the real premise of the speaker's words. In other words get past your emotionally charged reaction and seek to clarify the real message.

If the speaker is intentionally working your emotional or sensitivity side it will be helpful for you to slow the reaction tendency and clarify the words by simply saying "I confused, you sound; angry, hurt, upset. This allows you to step back from an emotional charged exchange; re-calibrating the message allowing you to start again to hear the speaker's words and intentions. This comment "I'm confused" gives them back their prior position and condition.

Process the entire situation and environment, don't react emotionally and don't take anything personally for in most cases it isn't about you - it's about the sender.

Evaluate the entirety of all factors in quick order:
- Emotion of the speaker
- Content of the message
- Intention of the intended or unmentioned meaning
- Posturing of the physical or angst in the delivery
- Attitude by voice inflection
- Inferences by innuendo

Active Listening

The best active listening communication practice is the ability to reiterate the sender's communiqué by re-stating what you heard in your own words and asking clarifying questions. If you're unable to do that, you're not listening.

Active listening is essential for successful, comprehensive and meaningful oral communications. This technique is a game changer when it comes to the word "understanding" and the age-old adage "what has been said and what have you heard." It's important to gain accuracy, clarity and mutual understanding when communicating. Active listening facilitates that.

I cannot stress enough the need to clarify all communications in any personal, business and selling situation. It is so very important that you strive to completely understand what is being said, whether you agree or not, and making sure there are no misconceptions in your understanding.

Make sure there is no doubt, no wiggle room for error, and no chance of a miscommunication between your prospect and you within the selling event. If you get it wrong, it will only result in more work on your part, less confidence on the prospect's part and more opportunity for your competition. You will never get it right 100% of the time, but an earnest effort will satisfy most situations.

Practice active listening with your friends, your family, your coworkers and everyone you come in contact with so it becomes second nature.

Let this become as natural as breathing when you are communicating with others and especially in the selling environment.

It's extremely important when you are in a competitive situation or stressful event to stay focused with your intentions and communication. The more natural you can make this technique, the easier it will be to become a great listener, the more comfortable it will be for your other party and you will become a better person in all walks and facets of life.

Don't be afraid to delve into and clarify that which needs your complete understanding. Your understanding is a prospect centric activity and is the underlying key to giving prospects what it is they want, what they may think they want, or what they may not know they could have. Don't hold anything back even if it changes the course of the initial direction. Reveal the entirety of your knowledge by communicating and clarifying your understanding.

Totally understanding prospects' needs through successful communication skills and respecting their desired result provides a great opportunity for you to show your capabilities regarding:
- Understanding their requirements
- Knowledge of industry standards and norms
- Your comprehensive knowledge base
- Use of forward thinking
- Effective problem-solving

Be communicative, be inquisitive and be enthusiastic.

Non-verbal Communication

There are so many books and articles written about non-verbal communication that I am not even going to attempt to delve into this topic, but mention it as a suggested reading activity.

I will say that it's extremely helpful for you learn some of the characteristics that make up non-verbal communication theory.

Your awareness will help you better evaluate prospects, their mannerisms and the telltale ways in which they are communicating to you without saying a word.

Body posture, eye placement during oral communication and facial expressions are the areas in which I suggest you become extremely proficient.

Written Communications - Business Compositions

In today's environment, written communication takes the form of emails, texts and tweets. The traditional written letter and fax communications are becoming obsolete as the preferred writing media.

One thing to remember about written business communication is that the reader is the internal voice as they read your communiqué. Additionally, because you're not there to facilitate interpretation, provide more information or influence their perception of what they're reading with an interactive dialog, your written expressions are critical. Use your words with exact and precise intent and avoid unnecessary verbiage and useless filler.

If a telephone or personal conversation would better communicate what you are trying to express, pick up the phone, walk down the hall or schedule a meeting to talk face to face. Written communication takes time to craft, proof, send, read and wait for a response. Would time and accuracy be better served using your verbal skills?

Written business communication skills are typically learned within the business environment and are enhanced over years of experience. You may also have been exposed to business composition writing while attending a school or university. Either way it's a unique talent that needs to be used and practice to develop effective results.

There are plenty of books that give examples and show how to form a business letter, a quote letter, a presentation, marketing materials, advertising, brochures, postcards and public relations communiqués. These are all forms of written business communications that may need your attention or crafting during your career.

All business communication writing needs to be exact, clear, concise, organized and to the point. The written word, paragraph, and entirety of the piece need to have meaning and not be filled with superfluous verbiage. Fluff is not enough; say what you mean and mean what you say by being exact in your writing and words.

It's imperative to have a logical and orderly progression or flow of thought within the composition. When the subject matter requires a series of events, times or dates, it is helpful to make sure your chronological construct is orderly and relative.

There may be times, however, when the letter contains multiple topics and varying issues that require organization and logic in relation to importance, timeliness or activity. Prioritize the subject matter in regard to the importance to the prospect. In these cases, it is important to be able to move someone completely through a specific topic or issue, transitioning to the next to show logic and forethought.

Choose your words selectively and avoid small, meaningless phrases, especially those that mean something to you and nothing to the reader. Avoid rambling on about a point or detail you have already made; those types of letters are ineffective and usually find their way to the wastebasket.

Always try to paint a picture with your words. One way to achieve this is to think about your written communication as visually as possible, actually envision written compositions individualized to the reader and use words that have an impact on and meaning for them.

Email

The unique thing about emails other than that you can receive them at work, at home or on your phone.

Effective use of the subject line, the first place a reader goes after the "from" box... just begging to be filled in with brevity and concise words to the point and action oriented when possible. Use it concisely to represent emails in a way that's compelling to recipients to continue.

The subject line is like a trailer to a movie, what's the next coming event. Another reason to use the subject line is some prospects will choose to index their emails using that well-crafted tag.

Yet another benefit is the fact that good subject line material creates familiarity and readers can automatically relate to the topic should they need to revisit the email.

The subject line also act as a differentiator, especially when you've sent multiple emails, allowing prospects to once again immediately relate the subject line to a material matter.

Keep in mind that on any given day, most businesspeople get hundreds of emails. And remember typically the identifiers of an email are your name, the date and time stamp and the subject line, so the subject line becomes a clarifier as it relates to you.

Under this scenario when people receive something from you in writing, they can always make a decision from what you have written and what is on the page, not having to deal with or speak to you. No conversation, no exchange of ideas, no interaction, and no, you didn't even get a chance to meet with them.

Solicitation Emails

If you're using emails to attract business without having a business relationship, the entire process becomes a very different strategy and a bit tricky.

Receiving such emails unsolicited equates to:
- Direct mail
- Door hangers
- Flyers
- TV or radio advertising
- Newspaper and Internet advertisements

If you are unable to catch the recipient's attention immediately, you will probably not be able to create any interest.

You may want to use email to just introduce yourself, let the recipient know something about you and your abilities in the body of the copy perhaps using bullet points. Also close with a note that you will call later. Don't forget to follow up with a phone call within 24 hours or you will be forgotten.

Meeting or setting an appointment should be the primary intention of sending initial unsolicited emails, nothing more. Perhaps use "Set an Appointment" as the subject line topic. To try and accomplish anything more than that may be a waste of time, effort and energy for you and potential prospects. Nothing really gets accomplished until you sit down in front of them and open a dialogue regarding business opportunities.

Another use for emails is in have another professional referring you as a professional. When attempting this have the referrer send an email introducing you to the potential prospect and copy you. Make sure they put your contact information is front and center, don't make it hard for them to locate (as in your signature block at the very bottom of the email). Any added comments and endorsements are wonderful to have but not necessarily essential.

Don't forget that the delete button is a private vote you will never know has been cast, so make your message count. You really want prospects to vote in your presence, and getting in front of them is the only way to ensure that. Nothing is sold by advertisements or marketing materials; salespeople make sales.

I always like to close all my written communications with a phrase I learned from a very professional secretary early on in my career with "Thanking you in advance." It has a nice personal touch, shows respect and is a differentiator from most communiqués. Feel free to "steal" this closing or if it doesn't resonate with you, come up with a phrase that does.

Directness

It is important that you speak or write with directness regarding any problem and/or opportunity that arises in your personal or business encounters. Many times we talk around what we need to talk directly at or to.

You are automatically invested in the outcome when you identify and pursue problems and opportunities with direct, honest communication. So take that investment seriously and stay in contention until resolution. Working diligently toward mutual understanding to achieve resolution through directness can circumvent hours if not days of dancing around issues, perhaps feeling hurt or experiencing unresolved turmoil that seem to want to linger without resolution.

Directness needs to have the elements of compassion, trust and respect for the outcome to be mutually rewarding and effective.

I believe most people want directness, both giving and receiving. Bring that candor and personal interest of engagement to your conversations along with your sensitivity and it will indicate to prospects that you are invested in the process of successful relationships and business practices.

And don't forget, tone is everything

Employer

Researching, interviewing and finding a worthy employer to showcase your skill sets should be a top priority. The market is flooded with me too salespeople who tend to burn out and move every two or three years between jobs or companies because of bad employment choices.

That does not need to be the case for peak sales performance salespersons. Finding a company with great products, branding and exceptional treatment of their people should be your top priority.

Even more important to you as a salesperson is a sales and marketing management team that approaches the selling event as a contact sport. By that I mean, any sport requires a sense of competition; in competition there is a need for coaching and skill set refinement to achieve peak performance. If you keep doing the same exhausting exercise and are unsuccessful you will probably either quit or move on. That is not acceptable to peak sales performers. Burnout, frustration and a no-win sales environment is not a good fit.

To determine a good fit is to approach the interview and decision-making process with a set of criteria that matches your professional desire. Below are some of those criteria I believe to be important in determining your professional future.

Company Mission

Whether you work for yourself or someone else, it is important to have a written mission statement that profiles business ethics, business intentions, and prospect satisfaction goals, combined with measurable criteria and results tracking.

As an individual business entity, it may seem unimportant to sit down and put your thoughts and ideas to pen and paper, yet it is a very useful exercise yielding a focused and committed mission statement. It's not just a statement; it's a mantra of purpose and intent that can serve as a reminder and motivation on a daily basis to perform at a very high level.

When employed, understand your company's mission statement, history, growth story, and culture are as important to your sales success as any other company component, including management, products, services, and other various resources. Having an understanding and belief in the company mission statement as it relates to conduct within and outside of the company organization helps represent and facilitate the company's commitment to its culture, surroundings, and employees, as well as their prospects' success.

Several key management figures or a group of selected employees typically write company mission statements. However it was derived, it is important to have a written mission statement in addition to mission objective and goals that act as a catalyst for behavior within the company and the marketplace.

If no written mission statement exists, inquire with management or other key personnel as to the intention of the organization to develop one. If nothing exists, it might be a good idea to spearhead a group to undertake such a task. Clarity brought by a mission statement with specified goals serves to direct the company's intentions and maintain focus.

If a mission statement exists, be completely familiar with every facet, either implied or specified. The mission statement becomes important to your overall company, product and service positioning activities and may be useful during the introduction of your company to potential prospects. Your practice of satisfying the company's mission statement will show your commitment to company policies and the desire to meet and exceed the stated goals and identity contained within the document.

Sales Management

One of the things that can hold successful salespeople back are overzealous or inexperienced sales managers that believe keeping close tabs on activity will yield higher productivity.

Well, it can as it facilitates burn-out or quite possible revealing a lack of trust or lack of respect that the salesperson knows how to do their job.

Monitoring number of phone calls, cold calls or appointments, ensuring all prescribed activity reports are delivered on time becomes burdensome at best. Additionally, attending typically useless and meaningless sales meetings to display and expose individual's performance in a team meeting is a show of power through enforcement and is not empowering to the individual.

Change the focus from activity monitoring to the mentoring and coaching efforts (10% activity reporting and meetings and 90% hands on coaching and mentoring) and you now provide the empowerment the salesperson needs to self-manage themselves showing your trust, respect and responsibility in their performance and development.

Using only the numbers as the key indicators is never a good strategy. A better way to determine salesperson performance is to have sales managers engaged in the coaching process, paying more attention to what is included in their activity and how the salesperson receives and applies coaching direction and information.

In most cases, modern day sales managers are poor coaches, managers or leaders because they manage the way they were managed, by the numbers and dictate the "perform to the numbers" process with little understanding of sound selling and sales leadership and procedures. Leadership takes energy and most mid-level managers think once they have arrived at their new station work is delegated to others or work to remove themselves from daily trench work.

Some sales managers hire salespeople who typically talk and walk the "proper" lingo and play their same game yet are able to show successful sales activity numbers from past employers. Numbers without sales is a reflection of past failures.

Most sales managers typically don't want to have to mentor, coach and train salespeople; they want that already contained in their new hire. Did someone say "seasoned sales professional". That's good, yet to evolve in the sales game you need to be kept current with the modern day playbook.

Some sales managers want to sit in their offices managing the numbers, make uniformed judgments on sales performance and blame salespeople for inactivity thus poor sales performance and never truly engage their biggest asset, their salespeople.

Stay clear of this!

Hiring of New Salespeople

As an evolved sales manager who believes in mentoring and coaching my first question to any new hire is "Why are you wanting to move?" or "What isn't working for you at your current position?"

These answers will indicate potential issues that quite possible reside within the salesperson themselves, the current company or their current job.

I want to develop people who want to develop themselves not a numbers driven auto-bot salesperson that is destine to burn-out a month into the job.

Once a new salesperson is hired, trained and up to speed on company policies, products and services, they are typically left alone to take on the prescribed and necessary activities, complete activity reports, attend meetings and deliver sales that have been laid out for them during the orientation.

Bad idea. It's time for new thinking and that resides around coaching the entire sales force, not just the new hires.

Coaching

Today coaching—which is different than training—is not typically a central theme for mentoring salespeople. Coaching requires one to be consistently in the field and in front of opportunities and the prospect while getting exposure to the competitor's savvy. This provides a continuous baseline for evaluation of their sales team's skill sets which can help them perform their job to the highest standard. This is necessary on a weekly basis.

Coaching and mentoring salespeople is a different skill set brought to bear on the selling process and sales managers need to be trained to be effective.

So, identifying the type of coaching you need as a salesperson and then find an organization with a manager that is evolved and willing to support your needs and utilize your skill set, capabilities and desire to evolve should be your top priority.

Sales managers need to understand the obstacles salespeople face including but not limited to external and internal competition; economic, political, and financial market conditions; and changing prospect dynamics. While these dynamics are real, inevitable and often in flux, they are typically not legitimate criteria when a salesperson loses an opportunity because of one of them.

However, it is imperative that sales managers understand the effects these conditions have on their team's mentality and coach empathetically on how best to develop the tactics necessary to overcome conditions outside their teams control. In most cases it's just a mindset not any action that is required.

Activity Tracking

I can't count how many times I've seen sales managers add two to three times more work in the form of activity tracking because they don't have the confidence that salespeople are doing what they are paid to do and what say they're doing.

In many cases, activity tracking is set as evaluative facts measuring one aspect of the job and therefore these metrics are typically set to manage to the low-end performers and a "lazy" mentality.

Peak sales performance is *NOT*:
- 60-100 phone calls per day
- 15-50 door knocks per day
- 10 good appointments per week
- 10-25 proposals a week.

The aforementioned is just busy work. Finding business opportunities takes finesse, solid networking, field and phone skills and a nose for revenue.

Peak sales performance uses a "work smarter not harder" mentality and is a successful balance of identifying real business opportunities and converting them into sales and revenue.

When I first entered into sales, I recall I always responded best to a couple of my sales managers who understood the need for metrics but also were compassionate enough to know there was more involved than just hanging on the phone and measuring the easiest activity by crossing it off or adding it to a list.

How many times have I heard "sales is a numbers game"? Yes, that's true to an extent, but without professional coaching, mentoring and training from experienced professional sales managers or support personnel, it becomes a long, drawn-out game resulting in frustration and inevitably burnout.

Not all salespeople are created equal, therefore an evolved sales manager needs to coach, mentor and train each individual to their own personality and learning ability. Most successful salespeople need to be in the field in front of people, working with their personalities, enthusiasm, and desire to inform and educate prospects about their products and services to win the business. The most difficult thing for an outgoing salesperson to be told is they must stay in the office so many hours a day to complete unrealistic numbers to support misguided goals.

I will examine in depth the management functions in the third *book 'The Full-Cycle Minute – A Construct in Evolved Management"* which is due out the third quarter of 2015.

Telemarketing

Although numbers of phone calls do yield results, it's usually not the strength of a professional salesperson, but a more appropriate task for a telemarketer. Professional salespeople are best utilized in customer facing scenarios that allow them to use their excitement to introduce their products and services and ask for the order.

It's necessary to distinguish the difference between a good telemarketer and a good sales professional. Most companies will not employ telemarketing people because they believe their professional salespeople should take on that responsibility. This thinking was established as companies downsized, while increasing job requirements and responsibilities of those who retained their positions.

Having a balance between inside telemarketing and professional salespeople in this day and age is essential. An appropriate mix of telemarketing activity and professional salespeople relieves burnout in both job categories and allows the skill set of each to achieve peak performance.

An example of such pairing comes from my experience I had while working for a newspaper which work very successfully where a "sale pods" philosophy combined a salesperson, an associate salesperson (telemarketing and customer follow-ups) and a graphic artist. These pods of 2 to 3 people with specific skill sets and balanced to a particular industry's marketing and selling activity were very successful. I've seen these pods obtain the highest level of productivity, job satisfaction and revenue generation. Typically this becomes infectious within the entire organization. The key to these pods' success is the strategic planning, tactical activity and execution of the plan. This group effort creates camaraderie and success in the collective effort to achieve revenue.

Marketing

Marketing is necessary function yet is an entirely different discipline with regard to sales and selling processes. Marketing is an essential part of the sales function yet in some cases it seems it's the tail wagging the dog. Too many times marketing aspires to drive the selling and sales function remotely, at arm's length from the field without knowing what is truly needed at the scene. One of my first mentors shared this with me; "anybody can make a product but not anyone can sell it" and "sales is revenue, everything else is cost" which still resonates.

I will say that marketing has a lot of influence on branding product, placement, price, people and promotion. This discipline is as varied as any yet in some cases marketing efforts in many companies lack the real understand of their immediate need to support field sales efforts.

Marketing efforts should have a profound impact on local markets yet a global strategy and focus are in most cases ineffective with regard to potential revenue.

Many marketing departments are fixated on the big ticket item of national and/or vertical industry advertising and branding. Most are missing the need for regionalized and even local marketing dollars and activity in well-defined field opportunities and markets. Needed is on-site market reconnaissance, accurate field business databases, local social media programs, targeted local advertising, effective direct mail and promotions while supplying an adequate budget and personnel to support such efforts.

Because the marketing function is a primary undertaking, discipline, function and activity a new book is being written titled *The Full-Cycle Minute – A Construct in Strategic and Tactical Marketing* and is due out the first quarter 2015.

My Sales Management Philosophy

During my days of sales management I had a very simple philosophy:

I will never fire you; you will fire yourself by your inability to maintain a high level of sales activity or a high level of sales production. Your inaction most likely will be reflected in a lack of results; sales is a results-oriented profession. If you're not producing and performing, perhaps you need to consider another career.

I always viewed the employees who worked for me as very unique individuals. The onus was on me to determine how I could best coach, mentor, and support them as well as interact with everyone to bring out their best.

That requires getting to know each as an individual and understanding as many facets of their being, including their character, education, experience, past career path, sales training, family life, professional goals and personal interests.

I believe in reviewing all my employees' personnel files when I take on a new sales or marketing department. While reviewing each file individually, I also would have a subsequent 30 to 60 minute conversation with each person to verify I understood what was in the personnel file so I could learn and understand who they are as a person and what I can provide for their success.

I would read the narrative reviews by past supervisors and managers, taking them with a grain of salt. Personalities dance in both opposition and agreement, so written reviews are merely the observation by one personality (the reviewer) writing an opinion about someone else at a specific time.

I was always appreciative of the effort put forward by the reviewer, yet I would always rely on my own personal assessment allowing a period of time while getting to know each individual.

If I wish to evolve, I too must allow others to evolve as well. By pigeon holing someone on past reviews or actions by another's opinion just perpetuates a stagnate design thwarting evolution.

Know Your Management Team

As a consummate sales professional and a talented individual, you are a desirable asset and you should work toward placing yourself and your talents on a quality sales team. When it comes to your ultimate job opportunity, your goal should be to join an elite organization, where you can satisfy your personal and career goals and objectives while evolving.

An elite sales organization looks different, as each individual sales professional is different. It's important to define your career criteria and match it to an organization that satisfies your professional desires. As a sales professional, surrounding yourself with an evolved, successful, competent, and experienced sales and marketing management team will enhance your opportunity for success while impacting your peak sales performance.

It will further serve you to acquaint yourself with the leaders from varying departments to broaden your resource base. This will help you further understand the intricacies of the company, its assets and its makeup—better preparing you for competitive scenarios.

Additionally, interacting with a variety of management team members helps you further understand the internal departmental and company dynamics, strategies and tactics that will benefit your knowledge base. By engaging the entirety of the management team, you become an orchestrator of all the company's assets while representing the company to potential prospects. These internal relationships will keep you connected to the relative internal situations affecting you and will render insight that will help you perform your work based on meaningful information.

Examples

As a professional salesperson, it's always good to have transparency into other departments, understanding of their challenges, processes and personnel. By collaborating with other departments, you will gain insight that helps you understand how challenges get resolved internally and how the solution may or may not affect you, your selling dynamic and your success.

I had an experience where I needed to understand management's challenges and the diversity of management strategies and tactics pertaining to a manufacturing concern requires understanding of the Finance Manager's challenges. The Finance team is responsible for the overall financial health of the company, including projecting capital requirements; controlling operating expenses, assets and liabilities; and keeping a watchful eye on manufacturing throughput in the form of inventory turns and just-in-time delivery.

The challenge for many manufacturing companies is to satisfy orders requiring short delivery windows while having moderate to long production cycles which can be compounded by a long selling cycle.

Sales professionals in a company like this should understand its inventory philosophies as well as its manufacturing production philosophy. Is the philosophy a "just- in-time" delivery that requires a concerted coordination of turning raw materials into finished goods, resulting in an immediate deliverable, or is it a "build to inventory" with a predetermined finished goods inventory level for timely delivery?

What you gain from this type of knowledge and information will not only help you set a realistic prospect expectation and impact your sales forecasting, but it will also help you understand what your sales opportunity funnel should look like to successfully contribute your portion of required sales revenue.

On the prospect side of the equation, it will challenge you to understand what the prospect indices are, such as preferred delivery dates, acceptance of partial shipments, desire for just-in-time delivery, or acceptance of overproduction of parts—all of which can affect the associated pricing strategy to satisfy diverse or multiple requirements.

As you can see, your relationships with other departments and management teams are necessary to successfully enhance your knowledge base, allowing you to satisfy prospect needs.

Yet another experience comes from a service organization that supplied creative marketing and advertising services. In this case, it was good to understand the Creative Manager's challenges regarding the existing staff that's already saturated with ongoing prospect demands and the selling strategy for bringing aboard new prospects without hiring new personnel.

New prospects being acquired within the advertising industry require a large allotment of account face time, hours and talented creative personnel to compete and develop winning programs.

The Creative Manager may determine that to bring on new prospects, the creative solutions portion of the account may have to come from an outside contractor because the in-house creative team is slammed. The Account Manager may determine they have enough account team to satisfy one more account and then will have to hire new employees.

Knowing that as a salesperson helps you set the correct prospect expectation and you have the confidence that your company will be able to perform the services required regardless of where the resources come from. That knowledge allows you to better understand all your cost components, in-house and outsourced, that affect your pricing strategy, creative resources availability, and ability to deliver a competitive concept and product in a timely manner.

Having a working relationship with the Creative Manager and Account Manager provides an understanding of the outsourcing strategy, outsource selection criteria or even the use of past consultants will enhance your confidence and help balance your resources between your in-house services and outsourcing to meet prospect needs.

In today's business and competitive environment, there are many options open to your management team with regard to satisfying the company's objectives and your prospect's needs.

This is why it is important to engage your entire management team and become as knowledgeable as possible regarding management's strategies and tactics, department functionality and the necessary critical assets required, all of which allows you to represent your company in the best possible light.

Become a Product and Service Expert

In becoming an asset to your prospect and company, there is a significant need to be totally knowledgeable and prepared with necessary information regarding your company and the products or services offered.

The selling environment is competitive and in some cases perhaps hostile, requiring a substantial product or services knowledge base to effectively procure business. Malicious selling scenarios can arise when the competition is extremely aggressive, desperate for business or just not able to competitively compete with your company on a product or service basis.

The competition may begin to take aim at your company's perceived weaknesses or your own credibility by using less than factual statements. Don't be sucked into that type of competitive scenario; stand tall in yourself, your company, and your product and services knowledge as well as your ability to compete honorably. Don't get rattled.

Use your team

Additionally, having strong company support creates a collective and personal confidence that will serve your selling situation and is outwardly discernible during your prospect meetings.

Take every advantage of all in-house assets to develop your product or service awareness and don't be afraid to bring additional skill sets from others with you into your prospect meetings. Sometimes including the president or owner can serve to represent how the company is devoted to prospects and prospect satisfaction by displaying the desire to earn their business at the highest level is necessary.

If you're with a manufacturing, Technology Company, or even a technical product distributor, there are usually plenty of engineers and tons of experience to draw from to help establish your product or service knowledge and foundation.

These are great resources to have in your back pocket when you're in the field and are confronted with questions you're unable to answer; support is readily available or just a phone call away.

Have confidence in these resources by relying on one of your greatest assets, the entire company. You're not out there alone.

Product Applications

It's important when you are looking for and developing new business opportunities to totally understand the application of your each of your products or services to the fullest extent possible.

With comprehensive product knowledge, you are enabling a better result while hunting for profitable selling opportunities. It's amazing how much time can be wasted looking for an opportunity while not understanding the company's prospect profile, product applications or target markets.

If you work for a company in the technology space, you need to spend time with design engineers, programmers and perhaps manufacturing engineers to really understand the depth of the company's products and solution set capabilities. Your company may have a standard product offering yet are you aware of a nonstandard product philosophy that requires certain criteria before it's offered. Knowing that, you may engage applicable prospects with another set of capabilities.

Understanding potential prospect requirements and then applying your company's versatility of standard and nonstandard solutions becomes a major competitive advantage. Knowledge of these attributes will bring profitable sales and satisfied prospects.

By understanding all your company's capabilities, you inherently bring a degree of confidence that may be unmatched by your competition. Regardless of what kind of company you work for, never be afraid to approach people in other departments with questions and concerns from you and/or your prospects. Always error on clarity; don't be afraid ask any question.

Additionally, if a prospect's knowledge of your products or services is lacking and you wish to inject more or better information, do not hesitate to ask a subject matter expert to join you as a complement to the undertaking. That action will be completely appreciated by your team members and the prospect.

Your colleagues will immediately accept and respect you as a team player and you will become an inclusive and collective part of the overall company team. This approach to create collaborative solutions for better understanding by all parties will be invaluable over the course of your career.

Prospects

It's interesting how the language works when the misuse of words, which is usually unintended, becomes a norm or standard.

Let's begin this section with a clear understanding and some definitions:

- **A Lead** - an identified opportunity, no contact
- **An Opportunity** - a lead that has been contacted and determined to have an interest in your product or service and agreed to a customer facing meeting to discuss conducting business
- **A Prospect** - an opportunity that has met with you, has ask for a quote or proposal and has set the next meeting; both date and time; has a higher than 80% chance of making a purchase
- **A Customer** - a prospect that has purchased from you.

It's from the prospect intersection that we will continue to view the necessary functions that can get your prospect to customer.

Know Your Prospect

Take the time to know your prospect and understand that your prospect interaction may not be limited to just one person or point of contact.

When there is a group effort and your suspicions indicate a committee may be involved, it's important to honor the collective approach and determine the decision-makers and the point person. It may not be just the individuals sitting across from you who represents themselves as the decision-maker; there may be others.

In some cases, the prospect may request additional participation from other company team members. This audience can provide perspective, expertise, and input to the evaluation and decision-making process.

These added individuals may be influential and may or may not make up the entirety of the decision-makers. Always check to insure you understand the make-up of the entire decision making group.

It's also imperative to know more about the prospects company entirely; its purchase objectives, evaluation process and how it desires to engage your company to solve a problem or satisfy a specific opportunity. Make sure you get both the wants and needs lists early on, prior to the development of your presentation.

Notice I said, "Your Company to solve," not "you." I believe if you broaden your persona including your company as a collective team and by distributing the sales opportunity across those who support you and the organization as a whole, your success will be less strenuous and more likely. Take full advantage of your team members and confidants.

Additionally, by showing a broad and united front across the organization rather than present a potential arrogant front of one you have displayed a comprehensive solution of your entire assets. Yes, you are prospect facing and yes, you have the sales responsibility and yes, and you have resources to utilize so go be the leader. It's incumbent upon you to orchestrate the assets of your company to satisfy the needs of your prospect, which will in turn satisfy the selling opportunity and processes successfully.

This holds true no matter where you work or what you sell. If you're selling anything, there's usually a company behind it. The company probably has more knowledge, more brand recognition and more branding than you, so maximize that to your advantage.

Identify Needs

Prospects need to convey to you what product or service features and functions they require, as well as quantities, delivery and any budgetary information they can provide before pricing becomes a part of the conversation.

So don't start at price.

Don't forget, they will tell you their requirement yet it's incumbent on you to evaluate that need and assign your product set knowledge to offer other solutions that satisfy those needs which the prospect may not be aware of. Your alternative suggestion may add the value differentiator needed to win the business.

One way to establish the requirement for product value is during the exchange of information for product or service requirements, developing the ability to have prospects definitively state their needs, recognize your company's commitment to quality, and agree with a requirement for quality and value.

What I mean by that is, if quality is a valued requirement and your products have the ability to deliver this requirement, ensure prospects agree that they need a quality solution by having them say that. Use clarifying questions: "How important is quality in your decision-making and why?" or "Is quality important to you and why?" Asking specific quality questions is also a good strategy: "Is mean time between failures (MTBF) an important and part of the decision criteria?" or "Would lower maintenance fees impact your decision?" "Is lowest price a criteria?" The more questions to clarify the better. I'm in favor of questions that are open-ended and facilitate discussions pertaining to quality.

Who's the Decision-Maker?

It's always important to determine who the decision-maker is, whether an individual or a group, as soon as possible. Your initial contact may be with a group or someone who has been instructed to gather information and/or interview companies with the potential to provide a solution for a specific opportunity.

Whomever you are in front of or speaking with, your challenge is still to determine the decision-maker. Equally important is uncovering how that person or the company makes purchasing decisions.

Initially, some prospects may decide not to divulge the decision-maker or make that knowledge moot by stating they are just doing research and collecting information as a preliminary step before entering the purchasing process. In these cases, you may need to honor that position yet you need to be relentless about finding out more about their process and the decision-maker information.

If you haven't found the decision maker but are working with the fact finder it's critical to treat the fact finder with respect while determining who the ultimate decision-maker may be.

It's important to meet with the decision-maker at least once prior to any presentation of any materials. This meeting gives you the access necessary to delve into how the decision will be made, including company policies, criteria, process and procedures as well as the final evaluation.

It will also be valuable to find out what bearing the organization has on the process and its strategy moving forward or purchase guidelines. Try to determine any special relationships with other vendors or competitors that may have a bearing on your proposed solutions.

Once again, it is vital to take the time to have meaningful and directed conversations that include product or service reviews and clarification of the sales opportunity. It's not a single conversation yet a series of questions regarding the decision-making process, purchasing procedures and ultimately selecting a vendor; it's about clear and concise communications that establish a professional working relationship. Take the time to develop a list of the prospect's desires and objectives.

You'll want to keep and track a prioritized list of the criteria expressed by the prospect. This list and other essential decision-making facts will enable you to make an informed decision on your strategy and the tactics that will result in a comprehensive, relevant presentation.

During this whole process, don't be afraid to ask questions, even those that might increase the scope of services and thus the price. Ask any and all questions. It's imperative to get the prospects' laundry list of features and benefits, desires and wishes, whether actual or fantasy out and on the table.

Once all the requirements have been aired, restate them in your own words while adding your company's capabilities to fulfill them. Again, your company not you.

Be a very good active listener and combine that with an effective process of questioning to get everything on the table. Make sure you don't intimidate prospects or cause them to become defensive during this process. Use a calm, controlled tone and demeanor.

You can come off threating if you're too push or appear to be aggressive. Take your time; be genuine in your processes and your work.

There are gentle ways of getting information from people by using proper tone of voice, a seemingly harmless question or by just being and using your natural inquisitiveness. These types of skills need to be developed for each individual prospect, or person, since all prospects and people are not alike. That's why it's important to understand how to communicate with the person sitting in front of you, decision-maker or not.

Ask Business Questions

During your interviews with prospects or decision-makers, it may be important to ask questions regarding:
- How the outside business climate and economic environment affects their company?
- How the cost of raw materials affects the business and identify which ones?
- How the local or national political landscape impacts their business?
- How the financial markets influence their decision-making process?

It's investigation across all lines of your business acumen and the current business environment that will yield the most fruitful information and insight. During this process, make sure the prospect has time to answer these and other business-oriented questions to your satisfaction.

The answers to these and other questions are important no matter if you're dealing with:

- A public company
- A private company
- A local, state, or federal government agency.

Typically, if you set up interviews with complete and comprehensive business environment concerns on the agenda, prospects will usually afford you the time and engage in the discussion.

Speaking of agendas, it's always good to outline a written agenda or present a verbal agenda prior to kicking off any meeting. It may be presented prior to the meeting or in the meeting. My preference is prior to the meeting, to give prospects plenty of review time and the chance to ask for amendments or necessary materials.

I'm not big on asking too many, if any, personal questions unless prospects intimate a desire to move in that direction. My belief is if prospects wish to share personal information or stories with me, I'm more than willing to engage them. I'll be receptive, respectful and may provide some personal information about myself, yet I'll usually wait until we've established more of a relationship before having any in-depth exchange. I'm all for personal interaction with prospects once I've established professional relationships with them.

I would warn you against using a set method, script or the old-school process of inquiring about pictures in the office. This might be recognized as a tactic and perceived as somewhat shallow. A better way toward a personal engagement would be to bring up something personal a prospect may have mentioned during your conversations.

A reasonable question or inquiry could reveal itself when prospects refer to visiting another of the company's facilities or a visit to another city or state for business purposes. Both of these are natural openings that give you an opportunity to demonstrate your interest or share a relevant story. I would use something like that as a point of departure so prospects sense your engagement with sincerity versus a relationship developed by a formulated process. In any and all cases, I'll always error on sincerity.

Listening

As I mentioned in the "Communications" section, listening is a critical element that requires a continuous effort to perfect, refine and continuously deploy.

Make sure you turn down the noise in your head and pay close attention to the conversation, the content and any unspoken inferences. Verify you understand what was said and make sure there are no misunderstandings or unanswered questions lingering in your mind.

An effective way to achieve that is ask, "Have I touched on all the issues and answered all your questions?", or "Are there any other questions you may have that we haven't addressed?" Be the detective you know you were born to be.

Verify Communications - Spoken or Written

Spoken

As we've already discussed, the best way to verify oral communications is to clarify what it is you think you heard by restating what was said in your own words. The best way to do that is to use active listening techniques, which were covered in the "Communications" section.

Additionally, it's always good to ask more clarifying questions, especially open-ended questions, which provide more than yes or no answers, and be patient with yourself and the speaker.

Written

Verifying written communication is as equally as important, especially in this era of electronic written communication in the form of emails or texting is predominate. Once a written communiqué is released, it cannot be easily retracted, if at all. Thus, be extremely careful with the content you communicate and especially sensitive to the tone of the message, which is reflected in your word choices.

An example of what not to do in your written communique might be:
- A communiqué constructed during a stressful time reflecting unprocessed thoughts and feelings
- Send un-proofed messages
- Mistyped or erred price
- An unrestricted embellishment you would later like to retract.

Just remember a ringing bell cannot be silenced. It may be better to take a little more time to really think through and thoughtfully compose messages before you hit the send button. Or, it may be better and more effective to either talk face-to-face or on the telephone to ensure accurate communication. Don't be in a hurry to send the wrong message.

Remember, verification is only the process to confirm what you believe you understand to be the facts and an understanding is void if there are any lingering questions. Error on the side of finding the facts and clarify your understanding by not assuming. Ask the questions, clarify the answers, and clarify your understanding while illuminating your prospect's desires thus satisfying your own need to reveal all the facts.

Redefine Solutions as They Change

I've always believed that when a course of action or target has changed, it's critical to acknowledge that immediately and set objectives for the new goal.

Although it may not be obvious to prospects, your knowledge base may be stimulated by a far different evaluation processes, resulting in a completely different approach or solution. It may be as simple as understanding what prospects are asking for in product X is only available by modification product X. The solution may resides in an existing product and is available in product Z as a standard feature.

There is an old saying, "give prospects what they want," but I also believe you have a responsibility to guide them through differing ideas and solutions, regardless of how you think it may impact the sale. Stay true to your Personal Foundation traits of honesty and integrity; they will always serve you.

Perhaps your new solution may have a larger price but have far-reaching and longer positive effects, satisfying an unknown or unspoken requirement. When I say unspoken, it may be something you intuitively sense or know, but it hasn't come to light in prior discussions. Sometimes those types of stirrings stimulate a more enlightened conversation regarding prospects' end requirements. I call that forward thinking, something that's essential to bring to the process and to fully explore and satisfy prospect requirements not evident in their stated desires.

This invaluable information may not only come from you, but from prospects through the course of questioning, dialogue and the pursuit of understanding their requirements. These "data-mining" conversations can stimulate different perceptions and thinking, revealing new requirements in a different light or direction without predetermination. In other words, it just may be something that hasn't been thought of yet. Part of your job is to push toward the desired solution, exploring and exhausting all thought processes and opportunities to satisfy stated or unstated needs.

By presenting a safe environment to think aloud, think outside the box, and promote the spirit of cooperative, interaction provides for relationship building, mutual respect and relationship longevity.

When you make yourself an asset, it's difficult to dismiss your process. Perhaps setting an agreement of agreeing to disagree to explore all options without a need for ownership or right or wrong is a desired point of departure.

Pace and Timelines

Setting a timeline for all future activities, including the delivery of your presentation, prospect product delivery date requirements and your ability to deliver the product on time is a key factor in many cases for choosing a vendor.

Additionally, pace and proper expectation of timetables are important with respect to your ability to properly research prospect requirements, meet with prospects, identify and meet prospects' time frames for delivery, and establish solution- building techniques necessary to help move the process along unobstructed are equally important.

Time is money, and the wrong solutions eat up time, opportunity and assets. And, a solution that is in error is not good for prospects or you. Thus, be mindful when setting timelines to allow yourself enough time to perform flawlessly while satisfying prospect requirements.

Set the proper expectation by doing the work of investigation, research and proposed solutions upfront.

One of the things that will help move the process forward is to drill down on how prospects evaluate their purchases. As mentioned before, knowing prospects' purchasing criteria and vendor selection process is essential.

The following questions will help set a pace with regard to potential obstacles that need to be overcome or satisfied before prospects are willing to commit.

- Are you quality driven?
- Are you price driven?
- Is there an existing vendor?
- Is vendor loyalty issue?
- Are you getting multiple quotes to keep the current vendor honest?
- Have you purchased this type of product or service before?
- Are you willing to sign a contract?
- Do you require a visit to our facility?
- Do you require references?
- Do you want to meet with our senior management?
- Does my company's time in business matter?
- Are you the decision-maker?
- If not, who is the decision-maker?
- If I'm able to satisfy all your requirements, will you buy from me?
- How long will it take to make a decision?

All these questions will impact the timetable of your successful sale. It's imperative to address all issues upfront and not let them linger until the back end of the process. The answers to unasked questions could derail the entire opportunity; it's best to know the entirety of what you're dealing with so you can be prepared.

Remember, a question not asked is a problem waiting to happen.

It's your responsibility to take leadership of the process. After all, you are the products expert and the one seeking to earn the business, so do everything you can to make that happen. Think of it as being a detective who is born with or develops an innate ability to keep digging until the facts are found. In the selling process, the only way to define prospects' needs is to uncover them through questions and an ongoing dialogue.

Another time-saving and timetable-impacting question is, "What did you like and dislike about your last purchasing experience?" A clear insight into what is imperative to the upcoming purchase will help you understand how prospects think, evaluate and operate.

Although you may have difficulty fitting this one in while seeking opinions, understanding any past experiences or nuances of issues may uncover potential issues that need to be addressed. It's important to be clear with prospects; they're not just there to evaluate you as a vendor, but to further understand how you can help satisfy their needs while interacting and functioning in relationship based on what's important to them.

Getting prospects to talk about their purchasing experiences will help you gain a better understanding of what makes them tick and build personal rapport.

Sales Presentation

Delivery of a written sales quotes can take various forms; a short form written proposal, a prospect driven specification requested by a formal Request for Proposal (RFP) or Request for Quote (RFQ) or a formal presentation using a laptop or laptop via overhead projector to present your suggested solutions, recommendations and information.

Sales Proposal

A sales proposal that satisfies the prospects requirements is a critical piece to the successful procurement of earning the business.

The proposal may take form as a written document that represents your recommended solution, and it can take any number of forms.

Suggest, if you have one, to your prospect the use of your normal proposal formats by showing an example and confirm that will satisfy their needs.

The written proposal and product information may be formatted in many various ways. The simplest is a written quote contained within a letter, typically with line items of product descriptions and appropriate pricing that is accompanied with standard terms and conditions and perhaps a cover letter.

Support documents may be necessary in the form of product data sheets or catalogs should the prospect request hardcopy material. If this information is available on your website suggest the paperless approach. The best way to present your written proposal is in a meeting allowing the review of the entire proposal and specifically the itemized products or services. This facilitates the necessary person-to-person exchange of information, clarity and negotiation process allowing closing the sale.

Prospect's Specification - RFP/RFQ

Some prospects may require more formality and require response adhering to a format outlined in the form of a RFP or RFQ solicitation. If this is the case ask if there is an electronic version which allows for expedience and less manual input. In cases where RFP or RFQ's are involved be alerted to the usual inclusion of their terms and conditions (T&C). Know that everything is negotiable so spend time reviewing them to ensure you're able to adhere to the T&C's and know you may be able to push back when unrealistic demands are made.

Typically RFP and RFQ have a required completion and submission delivery date.

One way to help insure your success is to write or help write the specification that will be presented to the market. There is nothing illegal about helping to write the specification.

Formal Presentation

In cases where there are multiple attendees and/or a large amount of material to present, a multi-slide format in the form of PowerPoint[1] presentation is quite helpful. This can be delivered in a small setting displayed on a laptop or to larger groups using projection equipment.

In any event it's usually a good idea to have a printed version of the presentation available for attendees allowing easy note taking or easy access if a revisit at a later date is necessary.

Your presentation should include pictures, drawings, tables, spreadsheets or graphs required to help your prospect visualize the solution. Visual aids are a necessity for conveying product form and function with not only hard goods but also non-hard goods such as creative for marketing solutions, artwork and copy which support the solution.

Placing a printed copy of your proposal in the prospects' hands reinforces what has been spoken and translated into a physical hard

[1] PowerPoint is the trademark of Microsoft Corporation

copy. The physicality of the deliverable presentation facilitates a form of ownership for the prospect. This leave-behind is another portion of the process to facilitate potential buy-in.

Making printed copies of the PowerPoint slides available during presentations is also a valuable strategy. Encouraging note-taking during your presentation engages prospects' physical, psychological and emotional connections to your proposed solutions with their immediate participation.

Upon completion of your presentation, as you move into the Q&A period, having the ability for the prospect to reference notes, clarifying and achieve understanding is extremely helpful to prospects. Having them flip to the page that represents the slide in question yet again engages them with a physical object rather than just words or a visual image.

Most humans are typically very tactile and once handed something, the exchange is a form of acceptance, a conciliatory act. Having the ability to touch the paper, turn the pages and interact with them is useful as a reference for prospects to hold and maintain in the current need and the future reference.

Proposal and Presentation Delivery

The delivery of the proposal materials or your formal presentation comprising the materials might become a topic of concern when it's requested that they're delivered absent of your presence. Prospects may request it be sent via email or dropped off so they can look at it when they get a chance and will address any questions at a future time.

Insist that any quotes, proposals or presentation materials be delivered in person, at a scheduled and with enough time allotted to complete a comprehensive review.

Why?

It is necessary so you can interact with the prospect and review all details within the materials prepared, determine and answer any questions that need to be addressed and identify any deficiencies once presented.

When you merely deliver materials, prospects usually skip to the bottom-line pricing, missing the value by assuming they know the content deciding to skip important information. Avoid that scenario at all costs.

Do not email proposals. You can overcome prospects' objections by simply saying the information needs further explanation and it's important that you are available to facilitate a comprehensive understanding. You also might say, if there is a large amount of material, that email is an ineffective way to disseminate such a large amount of data.

When prospects insist you forward a copy via email, I suggest eliminating the pricing component, stating you will bring the numbers with you to the scheduled meeting. This will only work if you have a definite date and time for the proposal review to take place.

When you schedule the meeting, set a solid date and time allowing an adequate amount of time for the presentation and questions; make sure you understand who will be attending. It's important to understand your audience and know how many copies of the proposal you need.

Make sure you know attendees' names and the roles they play in the company and in the decision-making process.

Remember, you've got to ask those questions up front, always ask questions, and always clarify. Knowing who you're about to engage is half the battle.

The Meeting Agenda

Prior to the set meeting day draft an agenda and gain sign off with you prospect. Set the formal itinerary that satisfies your prospect's requirements and supports your solution criteria for an effective presentation. Don't forget to confirm the time and date.

As an example, the agenda should include:
- Attendees Names (including your team) (Introductions 10 min)
- Confirm time allotment
- Presentation topics and time allotment per topic
    - Restate and reconfirm prospects needs (5 min)
    - Present proposed solution (15 min)
    - Product introduction (15 min)
        - Features and benefits discussion (5 min)
        - Pricing (10 min)
        - Warranty (5 min)
        - Delivery (5 min)
        - Terms and Conditions (5 min)
- Question and answer period (15-20 min)
- Ask for the order (immediately after Q&A; don't include this but be ready to make your request)

Make sure you confirm the prospect has a proper amount of time to actively and effectively participate, allowing you to complete your entire presentation. There is nothing worse than having confirmed a one-hour meeting, only to find out you can only have 15 minutes once you get started.

In that event, if the presentation requires an hour, opt to reschedule and allow yourself the proper amount of time to do your complete presentation. Being cut short typically will not happen, yet I would rather error on the side of knowing and regrouping than not knowing and trying to fit the presentation into a smaller time window.

Also make sure prospects are aware of the number of participants you plan to bring with you, allowing for the appropriate room size, number of chairs and available writing surface to comfortably accommodate everyone.

Additionally, it's important for you to understand how much of your company team support you'll require during your presentation.

In the event that a PowerPoint presentation will be given, ensure you know how to connect your laptop to the projector, have a working projector, an extra light bulb, and a proper backdrop to accommodate a professional performance.

Presentation Agenda - Introduction

Upon commencing the meeting and review of the presentation agenda allow for a brief introduction to introduce yourself, your guests, your company and its capabilities as well as any prospect guests. Don't forget to delve into your own relevant personal career experience within your current company as well as any pertinent industry experience that's relevant to the current prospect solution.

Also sharing the company's background, mission statement, and customer service and support philosophies enables prospects to gain perspective and an overview necessary for understanding your solution.

At this point, I like to briefly mention any product or service guarantees, warranties, and return policies. I typically won't put it on a slide at this point of the presentation, but will mention it to help facilitate a potential question downstream. Revisit product and service guarantees and warranties with a single slide toward the end of the presentation.

I would make sure all the company information you mention is contained in the proposal materials and presentation, including your own background. Keep it short and concise yet meaningful.

Restating the Prospect Goal

After your introduction and prior to starting the formal presentation, I strongly recommend you revisit and restate the general requirement and scenario of the product or service solutions requested. I would also revisit any agreed-upon purchasing criteria, such as a lease or direct purchase, potential order date and required delivery timetable.

Don't assume that any of the prior and mutual agreed-upon criteria and goals haven't changed. By leading off with this information, you can confirm the direction you have taken to satisfy their requirements or learn any new developments.

If you find anything has changed, be sure to make a written and/or mental note and if appropriate, you can make adjustments to your presentation on the fly or submit amendments later if necessary. Requirements may slide or move with regard to events, moving dates, or other acceptable minimal product or service changes that don't affect the overall deliverable.

Prospect Solution

Taking the time to detail and describe the selected solution prior to getting into specific products or services reveals with a broad stroke an understanding of the prospect's requirements. This is where all your active listening and detective work will pay off. You've already restated the product or service requirements, so the goal now is to delve into the solution based on the requirements you were given.

At this point, take a deep breath and move forward with your organized presentation regarding how your products or services will provide a solution that addresses the current opportunity. You'll be extremely excited to move forward with your solution, but it's imperative to pace yourself, talking slowly and deliberately while remaining calm and confident.

If you choose to entertain questions during the presentation, make sure you take your time to clearly understand what's being asked and formulate a clear and concise response.

Be aware of your conversational cadence and provide a slow and deliberate delivery, allowing for natural breaks and breathing in your speaking pattern to ease any tensions and facilitate understandable answers. There's nothing more frustrating than a run-on sentence that never ends or a person who's breathless but still trying to speak. By having an easy-going presentation style, you'll make the audience feel comfortable, letting them see your expertise and confidence on display.

I believe it's also important to make sure you're facing the audience and making eye contact as much as possible. I understand when you're making a projected presentation in front of a large audience and that facing the audience may be a little more difficult, particularly when in a darkened room. Plan for that by facing your audience, looking forward towards the audience rather than keep turning toward the screen, showing your back to the audience and making you more difficult for them to hear. Having the laptop on a podium in front of the audience is extremely desirable.

Discussing Features and Benefits

I suspect this may seem a little "old school" to you, but I suggest discussing features and benefits as part of your strategy rather than using a straight "value proposition" statements. It's from this vantage point that you can showcase the features and also connect them with relevant benefits.

Sometimes a value proposition statement is more like an unsubstantiated sound bite with no real foundation. The value proposition may contain a lot of information, yet it is very difficult to understand what it's based on or even how it's beneficial. A value proposition is just that, a statement, allowing you to "make a statement." That seems to be the only intent, not tying it to the immediate situation or requirement.

This is not the time at which you want to make value proposition statements. This is the time to discuss specifics that are fundamental to selling your products and services. Value proposition statements should find their way into your summation and closing portion of the presentation, after you have established the value.

Take the time to develop your product's features and benefits, tying the features to prospects' stated objectives or needs.

If during the product portion of your presentation, price is mentioned, don't get caught up in the pricing issue at this juncture. Defer that discussion to the pricing portion of the presentation by saying "I will address this in the pricing portion of my presentation".

The product portion of the presentation is also a time when you could start to hear competitive comparisons questions regarding your competitions' stated features and benefits or a comparison to your competitors' pricing. Defer the pricing until that section. Address the competitor's features and benefits. This is an opportunity for you to dispel or confirm what you know about your competitors with respect to your products and services. I would warn you, though, that if you're thinking of making any statements about your competition, make sure they're factual and you can back them up.

Support your statements about your competitors with a copy of the printed materials that pertain to their products and services. This information is available and can come in the form of a competitor's brochure or a download from its website. However you are able to procure it, make sure you have this "ammunition" with you if you are expecting to talk about your competitors using their facts.

Pricing

This is a point where regardless of the confidence you have in yourself, in your company, in your product, and in your presentation, you may become a little faint of heart.

If presenting pricing is nerve-racking, you need to revisit your mindset and thinking with regard to how you think about the value of your company, your products or services, and yourself. Perhaps you have not formulated or come to believe in your own value, your company's value, or the value of the products and services you represent.

Although price is only one component of the complete prospect solution, it can become an obstacle in the decision-making process if you haven't established a strong value for your pricing.

.

Once again, if you've done an effective job establishing the value of your products or services and the company you represent, you should be confident that your pricing will hold and prospects will be satisfied.

State the pricing with confidence and reassure prospects that it's representative of the quality of your solution and what they will come to expect.

Never retreat and lower the pricing as an initial recovery plan if price becomes an issue for gaining the business. If prospects want to change your price because they believe they can get the same quality at a lower price, you shouldn't avoid that conversation. This gives you an opportunity to restate the value of your offering and compare it with competitors that offer less value at a lower price.

In this situation, engage the notion that perhaps they could give up some of the qualities of your product or service to hold to their price point. In other words, are they willing to sacrifice quality for price? Your solution is priced to reflect the stated value of the features and benefits that satisfy the prospect's opportunity.

If you don't exude confidence in your value position and hold to the price, the purchase becomes about price only and not quality. It's imperative to keep focused on the value, quality and the prospects requirement satisfaction when having discussions surrounding pricing.

Remember, the best way to devalue your products or services is to lower your price immediately. There's an old saying, "if you sell on price you will die on price." Once you start down this road of conceding to lower price demands, you become nothing more than an order taker, not a salesperson who competes for business. As a salesperson, your expertise needs to include the ability to hold the value position and defend the quality of your product or service, not diminish it by lowering your price.

Another old-school saying is, "you get what you pay for," and that's all about quality. Perhaps there is a competitive savings now on their initial purchase, but there's a good chance that lesser quality products will cost the buyer later when they break down and require additional expenditures to repair.

You constantly need to remember and be continually reminding prospects of the quality of your product or service and its value to allow you to hold the price. Also, don't rely on basing the sale on a certain price point; live off the value of your company, your products or services, your expertise, and your selling skills.

Remember, price conversations are not necessarily an insurmountable conflict; you are just dealing with differing solution philosophies or value versus a perceived price point. Hold your ground and see where that leads. Don't project that if you don't meet a prospect's pricing requirement, you will lose the opportunity. It may be you just have more work to do, so do it and don't back away.

Price Contention

The surest way to extend the debate in this situation is to acknowledge prospects' desires and indicate that you'll continue to work to satisfy their quality demands and requested pricing. Ask for the opportunity, before their final decision, to be contacted to insure they have your best offer.

Responding in this manner keeps you neutral in the moment by not making an immediate decision or promise to satisfy their pricing request, and it will support your belief in your product's or service's value.

Make no indication or guarantee that pricing will change within this presentation meeting. Hold off any opinion until you're able to regroup with your team leadership for guidance or perhaps present an alternative solution at the next meeting.

There are some people who believe that closing the sale on the spot and having a strategy to drop your pricing prior to the meeting's end is an effective way to win the business. That is a valid tactic, yet in the long run using this philosophy broadcasts to your competition and potential prospects that your first pricing offer is not your best pricing offer and all they have to do is say they want better pricing.

Two things could result with this strategy: the perception of you and your company having no integrity while practicing situational ethics or the appearance of trying to rip off prospects by proposing a high initial price when you're quite willing to quickly go lower. Either outcome is not desirable.

Savvy and informed buyers will ask if there are any incentives or promotions available in this transaction to reduce pricing. I will always include those, but not until I have completely established my superior quality and value. Make clear to prospects that these savings opportunities have a shelf life, much like the expiration date of your quote.

I will typically make the quote expiration 10 days, which is equal to two business weeks. Shorter periods may be necessary if the prospect is known to and has a tendency to drag out the decision making process. Most company quotes are valid for 30 days, yet for me that is way too much time if in fact the prospect is serious about moving the transaction forward.

There are variables that comprise pricing in the form of costs that can change quickly in our current business environment, so it's important to not get locked into pricing that may not be profitable 30 days hence.

When asked to reduce my pricing, I tend to take it very personal, as if someone is asking all my colleagues and me to take a pay cut.

Why?

Because a lot of people in the organization have spent many hours building the quality of your products and services, completing costs analyses with respect to quality to determine the necessary cost components that comprise the pricing strategy. All those activities need to be reclaimed somehow.

I've heard it a million times that "The market drives pricing" or "It's a market-driven business environment and times are tough," so the expectation is to give prospects a break. All things being equal, I would love to be able to do that, but my greatest concern is for my company to be an ongoing viable and profitable business. Staying in business is paramount and it takes a reasonable profit to sustain ongoing and profitable business operations.

Having this strategic business mentality as part of your armor; it protects you from the initial salvo of dropping your price and serves as the logical position to hold the price point.

During any price reduction requests, work to understand your prospect's business practices; ask how they respond to a suggestion that they lower their prices without merit, just to give them thought for what they're asking for. You could phrase it this way: "Do you commonly lower prices without an apparent reason to satisfy your prospects?" On occasion, I've asked prospects that, but you need to be careful, as some will become defensive. Just some food for thought; use it at your own discretion.

Overcoming Objections

Overcoming objections takes a lot of patience and skill to actively listen to and understand the objection being spoken while hearing or sensing the prospect's real concern. Make sure the objection you hear is the real root cause of their statement and position and not something else. It's important to uncover the real issue or motive. In some cases, objections are a deflection from the real issue, so it's important to get to their root cause.

Overcoming objections is a topic that's covered specifically in many books and other publications that are available to enhance your peak sales performance. These resources will typically restate that you need to listen, hear the objection and take the time to formulate a meaningful response. There are many clever ways to overcome objections, yet the most successful way is to be honest with prospects and respectful of their intelligence; don't try to manipulate them with shallow explanations and diversions.

Here are a few typical objections that may present themselves during your process:
- Price – hold your value line, restate their quality needs, discuss the value of quality (breakage, maintenance)
- I don't have the budget – What was or is their expectation?
- We're decided to wait – Why? Get the real reason
- We're going to get another quote – Why, what didn't you like in my quote?
- We went with XYZ Company? What was the criteria for that decision? Why didn't you let me know before your decision, maybe we could have worked something out?
- You're a new Company – We are X yrs. old, help me understand how that could be an issue?

Every objection is different and unique because it's not just the stated objection, but any number of things: personality clashes, protection of an unfavorable reality (they like their existing vendor and won't tell you or they had a bad experience in the past with your company), or perhaps another underlying issue that is simply not being addressed or stated for some fear-based reason.

The biggest objection is what we just discussed in the previous section—pricing—and I really can't stress enough: "do not sell on price." You'll continue to get this objection until you find the courage to stand in your conviction of value with confidence, restating your value position as necessary.

Closing - Ask for the Business

This is by far the best part of the presentation because its where, when you ask for the business, you will get a concrete indication as to the prospect's thinking and the likelihood of you closing the deal.

My favorite question is "Is there anything you have heard that would preclude you from purchasing the product today?" or "It looks like we have satisfied all your requirements; let's get the paperwork started."

There are two things that will transpire once you ask one of those questions. You will get comments that sound and look like objections which could be stalling techniques or you will get solid input that will help you determine your next steps.

Let's talk about comments that look like objections and or stalling techniques. These objections could be exactly like those you have already heard and thought you satisfied. The problem is, in all likelihood you have not overcome the objectives and they're being mentioned again, so it's time to re-clarify. With that in mind, you need to start over by addressing their concerns. It's going to take patience and perseverance to find out if these are true objections or just excuses for not doing business with you. And the "you" I'm talking of may take many forms: your company, your products, or you personally.

The first two are easily recognizable. They can be dispensed with by revisiting and answering any and all questions, and with any luck, be quickly put to bed. However, if they're not the real objections but stalling tactics, you need to uncover the "why" and "what" of their position. After all, you can't do anything without relative or pertinent information, or in some cases the clarification of misinformation.

Wondrous things can be done with facts. Thus, work at getting prospects comfortable enough to divulge why they might be stalling. What is keeping them from being honest with you?

On occasion, I've had prospects confide that they're embarrassed because their process has changed or has been placed on hold; the objective has changed; or they've decided to purchase from their existing vendor and don't know how to tell me after all my efforts.

All those reasons are reasonably acceptable and you may still be able to work to put the train back on the track.

The "you" issue may not be quite as visible and is less likely to be exposed because it is a personality conflict or personal issue. I have felt on occasion I may be the issue in moving forward. Having been in this scenario a couple of times, I inquired only to find out that it wasn't me.

"How did I do that?" I asked. "Is there something I've done that may have negatively impacted your decision?" Yet another way to broach the potential issue and far more direct is to ask, "I see some trepidation and I'm confused because you appear to like the proposal, the product and our company—but would you rather deal with another salesperson?"

If so, there should be no difficulty in stepping aside and inserting another salesperson into the process if it means the company gets the sale. Accepting responsibility that you may be the problem or you may be blocking a sale, it's the right thing to do to step aside. After all, you're there to win the business, and if you're hindering that, you need to be willing to remove yourself. This practice facilitates a philosophy I live by: "I want to work with people who want to work with me."

Although times are tough right now, I believe there's more than enough business out there to be successfully developing and closing. I value my time and the quality of my work, so my time and work environment are important to me and I want to find fulfillment and joy my work. You should, too.

Provide Company References

When establishing a professional relationship with the prospect, I believe it's essential to provide company references whether asked for or not. As part of the initial leave-behind, I like to provide a list of current customers—company names only—in hope that the prospect may be familiar with one or two of them, which can add credibility. Make sure you have the company's permission before releasing any information including the company name.

When you get further into the opportunity and close to closing, it's important for your prospect to be able talk to one or more current customers about their experience with your company.

Always ask for permission from your references before you offer their information to a prospect and let them know they will be or are going to be contacted.

Try not to direct how your reference should represent you or your company, but you may suggest what might be important to the prospect. If you overcame an obstacle or conflict with your reference, sharing that with a prospect to demonstrate the way in which you were able to resolve issues would be important. Don't withhold challenging scenarios from your prospect that are good examples of creating successful outcomes through tenacity and customer service.

Take the time to explain your resolution process and share your ability to actively listen to any customer problem or issue and provide the necessary intervals for a solution, as well as how the solution was actually accomplished.

The more references that can provide solution scenarios to share with your prospects, the better chance there is of a trusting relationship being built. Take the time establish the extensiveness of your experience in resolution skills and the concern for a mutually successful solution for all parties.

The ability to resolve issues by utilizing conflict resolution skills is a great attribute to possess. Prospects will be glad to know you have that attribute.

Offer Success Stories

Without taking up an extensive amount of time, share pertinent examples of current success stories that will have meaning and apply to your prospect's needs and business.

Avoid telling stories that have nothing to do with your prospect's business just to have a story to tell. This practice is aggravating and could expose your lack of understanding of the current opportunity.

A perceived negative story can be a success story that highlights how you overcame a problem to satisfy a prospect and win the business. Be aware that the prospect doesn't live in "La La Land," where everything is perfect and nothing goes wrong. The reality of life is there is usually always a glitch no matter how small. Sharing your enthusiasm and indicating your resolve to satisfy and overcome any issues will say a lot about your Personal Foundation, your professionalism and your company.

Establishing Next Steps

Once the presentation has been completed and you have asked for the business, it is time to take a breath, relax any tensions and ask the prospect what their next steps are for moving forward.

Understand that very few sales are closed after the first presentation and on the spot, so be mindful of prospects' processes at the conclusion of your presentation. At this point, don't get too excited or pushy, yet be firm on moving forward.

Be aware of their timetable or process necessary to achieve next steps and get movement toward purchase fulfillment.

Prospects may not have thought that far in advance and are intending to regroup within their organization to determine and develop what they need to do next.

In the event that they openly acknowledge they're not clear what their next steps are, acknowledge their predicament and offer any helpful suggestions based on your experience with this situation. Recommendations to help them organize a logical progression based on your past experience or even providing a checklist for their review will provide comfort and necessary direction.

It will be extremely helpful to ask leading questions such as, "Would it be helpful to call you in two days after you've had a chance to review the list of next steps to set up another appointment?" or "Is there a chance you may need more information from me before you can make an implementation decision?"

It's important to not have any expectation in your voice that you are anxious to get an immediate answer or even the desire to close the business on your timeline, not theirs. Stay calm; this may be an important moment for your prospects and you. Perhaps they're determined to move in a fashion and manner that may appear conservative to your salesperson mentality but is necessary to them.

Stay patient and helpful until the process is finalized and completed. Stay in touch with prospects and if you have to, initiate contact when you haven't heard from them; error on the side of a fluid transition to facilitate completion. Never wait to hear from them; you are customer service until the products or services are installed.

Competition

A lot of salespeople know they need to spend time to develop their knowledge base on competing products, yet they do it halfheartedly. Unfortunately, from time to time, we believe we are aware of competitors' products or services, yet we only are aware of the basics or surface information. Having not completed a deep dive into the printed materials or website information, the best preparation has not been completed.

Having access to competitive materials that are available to the general public is helpful, but I also like to drill down further if possible and get the competition's support material. This can include installation manuals or service and maintenance manuals as well as any other prospect-facing material.

I also like to keep my ears open to gather information from competitors past employees and general talk on the street between salespeople. Occasionally, past or current competitor employees are willing to speak regarding their experiences with not only the company, but also the products or services they represented.

I'm not looking for covert material or anything illegal. Obtaining information from past employees' personal experiences can be very helpful to better understand the culture, product design or any potential problematic issues.

Gathering information about the competition is not for the purposes of developing a confrontational position or using it to discredit them with prospects. It's informative research to support an informed position about your competitors' performance abilities. Using information that relates to your prospects' beliefs about the competition helps you calibrate their perspective. I always want to be familiar enough with my competition to carry on an informed conversation with not only my prospects, but also my internal team.

By understanding your prospects' familiarity with the competition, your positioning statement with regard to your company and its products or services can be better differentiated.

You are in competition with not only your competitors' products and services, but the opposing sales teams.

It's important to realize how imperative it is to have a strategy to execute your sales plan with the proper tactics and not be caught reacting to the competition. I believe the importance is to know as much as possible by making yourself aware of their strengths and weaknesses as well as how they deploy them in the selling scenario.

Here's an anecdote from the world of basketball. I recall our coach saying that we need to recognize how our competitors' offense and defense are set up. In other words, when on the court, we need to recognize what to anticipate, to see or recognize next by the placement of players on the floor and the ball movement.

Offensively we would review their tendencies during our week's practice and be prepared to execute our defense appropriately. It was never a requirement to worry about it or try to control it, just be familiar enough with it and able to identify certain configurations so we could employ our practiced strategy and tactics. We knew our plan and didn't worrying about theirs.

This concept—you can't control it, just recognize it and develop strategies and tactics to prevail—holds true in the selling environment. When you're prepared, you'll respond with the process you've developed. When you're not prepared and are surprised, you'll usually react with emotion based on fear revealing the lack of preparation and process that could have been avoided.

Know Competitors' Strengths and Weaknesses

Like most people, when I think about strengths and weaknesses I visualize making a list and checking it twice. That may sound like something Santa does, yet it still applies here.

I suggest making a list not only of competitors' organizational capabilities, but also include products and services and their associated features and benefits. I would also add the management teams especially the sales and marketing team members.

Realizing that this is a lengthy process, remember once it's done all you have to do is update it when necessary.

Use a spreadsheet to categorize your company capabilities against all competitors by their business profile and then by their specific products or services. Competitors may have many products or services, so start with the products or services of your particular opportunity. Don't try to dissect every one of the products until it's necessary to perform that products specific competitive analysis.

Start by listing all your company's product features in a single vertical column and next to that, list the performance characteristics or specifications, next to the specifications list the benefits of each feature. From your last feature list any additional competitive features to complete the list.

A suggestion that will cut down on upkeep and changes is to establish individual worksheets in the same workbook for each company and link them (the information from individual cells) to a master sheet, allowing for comparing and contrasting products using one source, the master list.

Any updates or maintenance made to a company's individual worksheet will be automatically updated to the master sheet. The master is a comprehensive visual representation of salient features and benefits is easily accessed.

Also include whatever known current pricing information is available, including any discounting knowledge. Discounting and special promotions usually have a time element, so track those particulars as well.

It's important to have the most recent information possible and work under a "touch it once" philosophy. If you're going to take the time and energy to look up information, be sure to document it so you don't have to revisit that task. All you have to do is keep the list up-to-date and add new information as it's discovered.

Identifying the competitions' selling personnel is also critical, as that allows you to gain an understanding of the makeup of the potential salesperson dynamic and selling style. It's good to have established knowledge of some of their behaviors, strengths and weaknesses when you continually run into the same salespeople.

Remember all this information is dynamic; it will be under constant flux and change as competition, personnel, and markets become larger and more competitive.

Just stay informed and open to new information. Also be aware that in this day and age, campaigns of misinformation are becoming more prevalent. Thus, if you hear something, verify it with as many reliable sources as you are able; error on the side of accuracy and facts, not rumor.

Establishing Competitive Differentiation

As you compile the strengths and weaknesses of various companies and their products and services, you'll begin to see areas of distinct difference. It's a sound practice to incorporate competitive differences into your selling strategy, tactics and knowledge base, as they provide the fundamental differentiation within the selling opportunity. Retaining this information will provide a strong basis to develop strategies around competitive scenarios using informed competitive features and benefits as well as competitors' organizational profiles.

Having a strategy is important, but to have appropriate tactics is even more critical. Tactics will vary depending upon the nature of the situation.

A tactic may be as simple as not taking issue with an unknown variable until you have time to research it; or not responding to a misspoken fact or misinformed understanding without substantial support information, including documentation of your position. This is helpful when prospects recite information about competitors that may be wrong. Be ready to address these and other opportunities with as many competitive facts as possible.

Another tactic may be suggesting to prospects that the competitor supply hard copy information that supports the position, features and benefits or performance attributes that you know to be in error. Even better, have that information yourself and provide a hardcopy when possible. Whatever the tactic, ensure it is based on actual facts.

Preparation and facts are the key ingredients to developing a real-time informed response. This approach and work ethic should always be used to dismiss any misinformation.

Always work to gain a competitive advantage by using the facts; knowledge of your products and services rather than demeaning the competition. When presenting information that may conflict with prospects' thinking, it is critical to not come off as arrogant or as a self-imposed authoritarian but more so an asset working to establish a level and informed playing field that will satisfy prospects' required needs.

Be enthusiastic about getting to the bottom of facts and undisputed reliable facts. The facts are an important ingredient of the process of extracting and demanding the best from yourself and as well as my competition.

Adjustments to Maximize Peak Performance

When you are committed to evolving, you are constantly making adjustments to your very person, nature and profession. Your evolution is stimulated by the environment, people and information sources which affects our thinking and behavior.

By using the fundamentals introduced in The Full-Cycle Minute model, you will find that fine-tuning your peak sales performance processes and thinking will become relatively effortless and second nature. Just by being aware of the process allows for openness for change and improvement. Evolving your being also evolves your humanity and your collective way of life.

Your peak performance adjustments are as important as keeping any tool or capability well-honed and available for use. This pertains to not only your immediate selling opportunities and specific profession, but also your personal life.

It is helpful to understand and manage these personal adjustments by assigning them a priority and a reasonable amount of time to accomplish the desired change and outcome. It'll be helpful to start with small changes to gain successful events and the feeling of accomplishment while experiencing the process over short periods of time. Once you've accomplished these small changes, it'll be time to progress into moderate to large-scale changes to evolve in the directions you desired.

In many cases, to accomplish larger changes will require quiet time, reflective time, or being still over long periods (weeks or months) of time. In the case of undertaking a new event such as higher education, certifications or a dramatic career move, it may be necessary to assign even longer periods of time.

In cases of dealing with uncomfortable or unresolved situations of complexity, or the origin of your past thinking may also require a length of time as well.

Both situations require open, honest thinking as to the nature of the goal and the necessary resources required.

In cases of closely held personal beliefs and opinions, it may be necessary to revisit the origin of that thinking to reveal the very nature of it. Entertaining the idea of outside counseling or coaching can be helpful by having a safe place to discuss uncomfortable subjects. Remember any action you take is an investment in you and your future. Taking the action moves you closer to the outcomes you desire.

This process is not about blaming anyone or anything; it's about getting clear of the events or opinions that have transpired in the past that affect your perspective and opinion. The Full-Cycle Minute model allows you, as an evolved person, to use your new vantage point to revisit, reevaluate and perhaps draw a new reality or facts from those past events or currently held opinions.

This process takes a strong individual using honesty, self-awareness and an openness to a new reality to facilitate shedding old dogmas and perhaps unreliable belief systems.

By revisiting and evaluating your present day thinking regarding your history, thinking and your power to evolve a new beginning will and can emerge to help facilitate integrating your evolution into new thinking, desired behaviors and evolved outcome.

An effective way to accomplish the end result is to break the desired personal adjustments into three different category time frames:
- Immediate (small changes within a 1 to 3 weeks)
- Midterm-moderate changes within 6 to 12 months
- Long-term (large changes within 1 to 3 years).

Setting up the timeframe for any goals and desired changes is brought into reality and affected by a written list describing the type of change or goal desired and assigning a reasonable timeframe.

Looking at the ultimate goal and working backwards helps develop a clear-cut path of activity, actionable items and potential obstacles to success. It is critical to identify any and all elements that will affect your success or placate your goal.

Look at long-term goals first and prioritize them in relationship to amount of time necessary, financial requirements or outside resources that may be required.

An example of an outside resource would be the necessity to attend a school or classes. Ask yourself, "Will I get help from my company in support of financing, time off or mentoring?" and "Would this successful long-term goal yield a promotion or advancement?"

There are many other questions that would fall within a long-term goal evaluation. Make a list of where you want to be and what you want to accomplish in the next one to three years.

An example of a mid-term goal might be adding more prospects to your existing book of business, joining an active networking group, attending more industry functions, reading salesmanship books, becoming a mentor or finding a mentor. Once again, I would construct a list and prioritize your goals as well as track your successful accomplishments.

An example of a short-term goal might be making more contacts with potential prospects using the telephone, taking a two doors down approach (make contact with potential prospects two doors down after any scheduled appointment), or spending more time familiarizing yourself with your products and services.

It's critical to realize and recognize that with everything just mentioned, there is no mention of earning any money, only the successful completion of the identified actions. Any monetary goal is not a part of adjusting or advancing anything in your peak sales performance. Your peak performance is all about you taking action on items and/or issues you have identified that need to be adjusted to evolve your sales performance.

You can only affect the outcome by being prepared and taking action. The process to move forward toward your wants or needs is supported by self-awareness, adjustments and reflection based on your personal desires and honesty with yourself. Your honesty will help you embrace your authentic self, new possibilities, and new solutions that will require you to take action to ensure your evolution. Engage your desires, challenge your boundaries and limits, take action, and be alive and awake every moment of your life.

Remember, money is the reward or byproduct for a job well done. Money is not the goal or end result; if you make it so, it will continue to be elusive, for there will never be enough. Chasing money is a shallow way to measure your success. Material gain without fulfilling acts of humanity results in an unfulfilled measurements and a very empty narrative to your life.

The Dynamics of a Selling Day

One the biggest challenges we all face on a daily basis is managing the restricted of the number of hours in a day, more importantly, the 8- to 10-hour business day. Within those confines, you must determine how you spend your time, who and what gets your attention, and if your decisions yield what you desire and measure as success. Not every daily event will yield the aforementioned so you will need to work through those hours or days with a can-do attitude.

Sales success is very much about timing. With that in mind, selling is also about momentum. It's been my experience that most salespeople, companies and sales managers don't grasp that concept. Momentum is a rhythm that allows salespeople to be unobstructed by exterior minutia, unnecessary tracking or reporting as well as unnecessary meetings that waste time and are distractive to the sales process.

Most successful salespeople understand the need to build on the last successful sale, one sale at a time. With that rational, top performers build upon quick opportunity identification, taking timely actions and establishing strategies and tactics to convert opportunities into sales.

Selling Rhythm

The dynamics of a salesperson's day are individually different as each salesperson is unique, and as dynamic or submissive as a sales manager may influence. Know and set your rhythm that best suits your desired outcome.

Take the time to be aware of your personal skill sets, strengths and weaknesses and plan your day appropriately. It's easy to self-sabotage a day by creating excuses and claiming that what is being asked of you is stupid and you will do it but reluctantly. That mentality will never get you to peak sales performance.

It's okay to have excuses as recognizable and preliminary thoughts, but it's essential to move past them immediately and get on with the actions you need to take to fulfill your job, your goals and most importantly, your personal desires. The day is a gift, it's the present, so open it with enthusiasm and excitement.

Complexities of the Selling Month

There are number of indices that are used to manage a company's internal health and they are typically monitored on a monthly basis. The sales department is the critical mass that reveals not only the health of a company, but also carries the financial onus squarely on its back.

As you know, the selling month is a big deal for your company. The measurements of performance and indices used to determine the success of a month are many and vast. Included are the sales backlog (orders in-house), outstanding quotes with the probability of successful closure, sales activity logs (phone, appointments and networking events), product shipments (revenue) and services billed (revenue) as well as the general feeling and wellbeing of the sales team (full complement of hired sales personnel).

If things are good for the local, state and federal economy, then you might anticipate good sales. Conversely, if the cost of money is high and unemployment is high as well, this could indicate an extremely competitive and slow environment.

A properly trained sales team provides a set of professional eyes to the outside world with regard to prospects' buying needs and trends, products and services interest level, and a microcosm of the local financial climate.

Other outside influences could include the political mood and tone of the country or local market; the stability of the local, state and federal government; as well as seemingly unimportant weather conditions.

Management is always working to maximize revenue while keeping a close eye on sales activities; by sales team and individual salespeople. While the metrics for this is typically monthly, sales micromanagers will look at the numbers daily.

It's important to realize you eat an elephant one bite at a time. That bite is every day and the elephant is the month. While management is focused on monthly activity, your best success will be keeping your focus on what you do every day.

There typically is extreme pressure on the sales and marketing management teams to not only forecast their daily and monthly numbers, but also hit them consistently. These company goals are the cornerstone for the ongoing health of the business.

Every calendar month is different with regard to number of actual workdays as well as how often employees are out sick or on vacation. These variances in monthly dynamics will not usually impact monthly sales goals, but could affect the general company climate and the sales department performance.

Never use the inequity in the number of monthly selling days to make your case for not hitting your numbers. You'll just have to adjust to make up for any days lost, something you can do by better identification of sales opportunities coupled with more selling activity.

There are both internal and external forces at work that you need to be aware of as a salesperson. Not all of them will affect you; how you interpret and respond, not react to these indicators is how well you will move through them and toward your goal.

A Realistic Sales Goal

Management will set the sales revenue goals it wishes to attain along with the assets required for success. Your job is to take those requirements and formulate your own microcosms for your daily activity and actions. Plan your work and work your plan.

If you're new to the selling environment, you may want to engage your sales manager and/or other successful sales colleagues in your organization to help you set up realistic and attainable expectations. Sales management is also a resource for you to engage additional coaching and ongoing conversation regarding activities that yield successful outcomes.

When asked to do something you're not familiar with, such as undertaking a new sales position, take the responsibility to learn as much as you can from whatever resources are available. This includes asking people you respect how they might go about achieving success if they were in your position. Typically, those of whom you would ask for help will have a good idea of how what they would do in your shoes. Never be too proud to ask for help.

Additionally, if you're new to the sales profession, it may be prudent to find an approachable and helpful mentor within the organization to help you develop knowledge of the company, its culture, and its products and services. For this to work, the mentor needs to take an active interest in you and perceive your sincerity to improve your position and do what's necessary to be successful.

At the beginning of this relationship, you need to clearly state your desired goal for this mentoring relationship. This resource will prove invaluable. You may even want to go outside the organization if you have found a mentor that will commit to your philosophy.

For seasoned sales professionals, the key to goal setting is to understand what is requested and required of you by the company and your sales management team to meet your goals. Once that is clear, it is up to you to obtain those goals by any means, providing they are within the guidelines of company policy and procedures.

Even seasoned sales professionals need mentors and coaches as well, so don't be shy. Reach out to find either and take maximum advantage of any and all of your company relationships.

Lost Business

The lost business report can be extremely important and useful for uncovering trends and personal scenarios. When unsuccessful sales are encountered, it is imperative for salespeople to generate a lost business report. If one does not exist within the company, it is on you to start your own reporting system.

Start by tracking the following:
- General reason for lost sale
  - Price
  - Non-competitive product set
  - Product availability or delivery
- Elapsed Time
  - From identifying opportunity to quote
  - From quote to purchase
- Mistakes with
  - Gathered information
  - Quote
  - Proposal
  - Presentation
- Personality issues
- Timing
  - Not a real opportunity
  - Not ready to purchase now
- Changed their mind because of
  - Economy
  - Company financial conditions
  - Moving or closing down
  - Political

This system will yield unidentifiable trends not normally tracked in the business environment and in your selling process and strategies. Identifying any undesirable trends is necessary to correct sales losses and increase your success.

Lead Generation

Lead generation is the salespersons illusive nemesis. Why? Because leads generally don't fall out of the sky, appear on your desk in the morning or appear to you in your dreams. So, where do leads come from? Your company may provide them, you may purchase them or like most salespeople you have to work for them. With that being said here are some successful ideas I've used in the past to turn on my lead generation.

Networking

Networking is a very viable activity and the highest priority to grow your immediate sales opportunities while developing meaningful business relationships. Like anything else, there are good networking groups and poor networking groups.

What you wish to accomplish in your career is paramount, but most salespeople are interested as well in developing themselves socially as well. The social aspect typically go hand-in-hand with sales professionals yet staying focused on the professional networking aspects will serve with greater success and help you achieve peak sales performance.

Joining networking groups that focus on consummate sales professionals' desires to help each other become successful is imperative. These are many great groups to associate with yet finding a focused group that shares real leads can be a challenge.

First, find a group or groups that have an opening for your particular industry or products and services within geographical areas you are able to serve.

There are professional networking groups that meet after work, in a more social and informal surrounding, often with no unique geographical or industry requirements. My experiences have been they are more like happy hours than a forum for true professional business opportunity exchanges.

There's nothing wrong with that; go and have a little fun with the proper understanding of the outcome.

What is interesting, however, is that these events can end up being extremely time-consuming with little or no result. Attending may not get you any closer to your goals—but it will empty your wallet, empty a bucket of time in your day and perhaps leave your frustrated in the group and yourself. I would suggest you keep your social hours separate from business endeavors so you can relax and recharge your batteries while keep professional networking events focused on growing your business and revealing sales opportunities.

Don't forget that one of the most viable networking opportunities may come from your association with schools or institutions you have attended. That can either be a university or trade school, your high school, and don't overlook any of your military connections if you served. Any entity with which you have a past association is a brilliant networking resource.

Formal - Professional Networking

The more formal networking groups will typically meet in the early morning over coffee or perhaps breakfast to exchange sales leads. Occasionally they will meet at lunch, but most salespeople want to get the maximum out of a day and a midday meeting can be an interruption to their selling rhythm.

Typically, the group will be well organized and have an agenda for the meeting. Activities may include one of the members giving a talk on the topic that is important to the group, mainly sales and selling, or an introduction to their industry or profession, including products and services.

If you are in a large metropolitan area or an area that has distinct geographical areas, it will be worthwhile to find such networking groups by region as most are set up in that manner. The only potential issue is if the day and time the groups meet conflict.

Other formal networking opportunities may come in the form of online sites by that allow you to showcase your professional information. There are several websites that facilitate these types of exchanges and they have proven to be helpful and successful. Sites are being added daily, so be sure to check the web occasionally for new additions.

There are also online sales lead exchanges as well as pay-per-lead opportunities. Although I've yet to see a successful online lead exchange program, it seems there are new developments occurring. Check my blog at http://fcm-sales.blogspot.com for any new information on my website: www.jeffreyaharrison.com.

The pay-per-lead opportunities are expensive and somewhat unreliable when it comes to the impending selling opportunities. At issue is the timeliness of the opportunity as well as how many other sales professionals in your area have signed up for the same service, looking at the same opportunity.

I've never really made the effort to use my limited time and energies to buy unknown seemingly commoditized leads for the purpose of my success. I believe it's like trying to shoot a bear with a shotgun; the action has little effect except to anger the bear. In this case, the bear (prospects) are bombarded by salespeople who have purchased a list and contacted them with the same selling intent—and the opportunity may be old or already satisfied.

I believe it is important to be active within the marketplace, to meet people face-to-face and to knock on doors as another means to reveal and uncover business opportunities.

Informal – Interest-Based Networking

These informal networks are probably less sales professional specific and based more on a personal desire to achieve relationships with people who share similar interests. This networking endeavor may yield a completely different business professional, resulting in developing personal relationships with like-minded professionals.

In this type of networking, you may be meeting upper and middle management professionals as well as business owners or local government leaders and officials. Realize that you're coming together not to sell them anything, but to share your common interests, so be mindful of the appropriate time to broach a professional relationship.

This networking may come in the form of volunteering your time, talents and passions for certain causes or it could come as an interest in a preservation group that has a deep interest in keeping alive your particular passion or interest within your community.

These groups can be as varied as your interests, so don't limit yourself; you may even want to go outside your comfort zone to gain more and varied interests. It's a great way to meet new people and socialize with other professionals sharing common goals.

Business Referrals

There are several ways to get business referrals, yet I think the most important means is asking for referrals after you've completed a successful business transaction. It's a common practice to think this should be an easy proposition, gaining referrals, but it's more difficult than you can imagine. In most cases, prospects will be glad to refer you but have:

- No one to refer you to
- Don't have the time
- Completely forget their offer to refer.

Asking for referrals - during your presentation

Asking for and getting referrals is difficult at best. It becomes even more difficult if this is something you haven't mentioned during the selling process and the end of your presentation is the first time they are hearing your request.

In this case, the preparation for asking for the referral early in the next steps section of your presentation plants the idea and notifies prospects of your intent to ask for referrals later.

Mentioning it at that point prepares them to hear the request when you actually ask for the referral. Remember, it's setting the right objective about every element in the selling process that will yield favorable results. In my experience, no one likes surprises, no matter how small.

I would introduce it with a question: "When I am able to successfully provide the products and services you are looking to acquire, would it be possible for you to give me a letter of recommendation and/or a personal referral to anyone you might know who is looking for similar products or services?" This could come early in our first couple of meetings then a reminder at the closing.

These referrals are valuable and should prospects provide you with them, it is generally acceptable to provide a reward of some nature. Some companies, upon receiving a referral, will offer discounts if there are continuous services being purchased. Check with your management team to see if there are any such incentives or a rewards program that would benefit you and your prospects. I usually provide a small token of my appreciation for referrals—a coffee card or gift card—if a company program does not exist.

Other referrals

Referrals from friends, family, and organizations you're affiliated with will build your network and complement your selling efforts. It can happen as innocently as meeting new people or friends at a party, sporting event, or your child's soccer game.

It's important to remember that if you're personable about what you do for a living and are open to hear what other people do, you'll find selling opportunities you might not have uncovered otherwise. It's not that you're selling 24/7; you're just mindful of how business works and how you can discreetly discover sales opportunities in your personal life.

If you have a significant other or spouse, they are also good resources to help you identify business and selling opportunities. Again, it's not the primary function of any relationship, yet it can become a useful byproduct if handled in a respectful manner. The key is not to force it, but to let it reveal itself naturally both to and from you.

Professional Growth

As you review your professional sales career, it's imperative that you identify and recognize an acceptable and desired path that will get you closer to your career goal. I say acceptable because in some cases others who may have influence on you may have an idea for your career that might not be acceptable to you with regard to your timeframe, the need for additional education or the effort required for the desired outcome. Ensure you make an informed and conscious decision, one that isn't the result of outside influence or pressure.

It may be that your career goal is to progress into senior management as a General Manager, CFO, CTO, CMO or CEO. Or you could have your mind set on mid-level management, such as Sales Manager, Marketing Manager or Business Development Manager.

With these mid-management and senior management goals in mind, it is highly likely that you may or will need to acquire additional education. This can come in the form of a college or university course of study or specialized classes for the advancement into management. Other options may be certification programs or even position-specific programs facilitated by other professional associations.

Additionally, practical experience in supervisorial positions, leadership positions and other management experiences will prove to be useful in obtaining your goals. Take every opportunity to align yourself to as many leadership roles as possible. Although they may seem to be minor undertakings, it is always good to start accepting responsibility within volunteer groups, clubs or your local community as a way to build your leadership credentials.

Start developing your decision-making and leadership skills as early as possible to help develop your career path to obtain your goals. Take every opportunity to learn and grow from every experience that presents itself and interests you.

Also become extremely aware of the leadership characteristics of managers you appreciate and would like to emulate. This may not only come from your current internal management team, but also when you're sitting across from managers as prospects in the selling scenario. Make yourself aware of how they conduct business and where their style and process may intersect with your beliefs. Compare and contrast until you find the balance you need for your success.

There's never enough time to find good examples of management leadership and decision-making process to start to develop your own style. As long as you are open to the observation of quality management, concise decision-making and leadership dynamics; they will reveal themselves.

Additionally, if you're lucky enough to find a mentor, you will have found the pot of gold at the end of the rainbow. I would recommend you cherish and nurture that relationship for as long as you are able.

I was fortunate enough to have two wonderful mentors. One was inside our organization and held the title of General Manager and the other worked for a company outside the organization as the owner of a high-tech advertising agency. I enjoyed those relationships for a number of years and I still recall the many lessons I learned from both of them.

Stay open, stay available and keep evolving. Best of luck to you on your journeys around the Sun.

<u>Conclusion</u>

In order to reach your peak performance and become the best human being you can be you first have to be honest with yourself. Honest introspection and reflection will give your life meaning and direction allowing you to evolve into the best person you can be. It will also provide a pathway to an evolved life encompassing happiness, good health and a satisfaction that your choices are based in the fact that you are willing to look at who you are, what you are and whose you are. You've been blessed with a life on this planet don't sell yourself short and take every opportunity to add quality to your life and to others.

If you can't be honest with yourself you can't be honest with anyone and that presents a problem. In order for you or anyone you know to evolve it has to come from honesty within and honesty projected.

For if you're not being honest with yourself, your words and your behavior than perhaps you're living a lie. I don't think anyone wants to live a lie for it serves no purpose. A wise person once told me, my mother, that "when you cheat you are only cheating yourself". That sage advice is been a cornerstone to my character since that conversation.

You can choose to do your very best in every moment or you can decide to just do enough to get by. For to do your best takes energy, effort, commitment, and desire to affect any outcome.

Take the steps and the time to become great and not perfect; evolve don't mature and above all to thy own self be true. We only go around once so make it an evolved journey that fills you with happiness, joy, respect, decency and grace.

May the winds always be at your back...

Made in the USA
San Diego, CA
15 September 2014

16328847R00078

Made in the USA
San Bernardino, CA
29 October 2014